19 RULES

FOR GETTING RICH AND STAYING RICH DESPITE WALL STREET

19 RULES

FOR GETTING RICH AND STAYING RICH DESPITE WALL STREET

E. ALY

Marshwinds
Press Company

ISBN 978-1-7341170-2-8 (Hardback)
ISBN 978-1-7341170-3-5 (Paperback)
ISBN 978-1-7341170-4-2 (epub)

Library of Congress Control Number: 2022912469

Subjects: BUS027030 Business & Economics/ Finance/ Wealth Management

Investment and Book Clubs virtual readings and Q&A sessions are available by contacting:
Marshwinds Press Company
P. O. Box 21099
St. Simons Island, GA 31522
1-800-343-3751

OR go to **uniquereads.com**

Printed in the United States of America

Cover & Interior Design: Creative Publishing Book Design

For Judy,
who makes it all possible.

Contents

PART I

YOUR EXPECTATIONS AND PERSPECTIVES

Understand These Facts

You are about to find out how to get rich and stay rich despite Wall Street.

1. You will learn the principles of building wealth without compromising your lifestyle.

2. You will learn how to grow your wealth throughout the years.

3. You will see your income for compounding your wealth increase the longer you maintain the program.

4. You will have more and more economic flexibility in your life as you maintain the program.

5. If you follow the program, you will have a retirement unencumbered by financial stress from having to guess if your money will outlive you.

The ways Wall Street and their media enablers create an environment for speculating and gambling are described in this book. The discussion may appear critical; however, that's not the intention. Without the volatility from speculators' greed and fear, investors wouldn't have as many opportunities to find good investments at fair prices. Wall Street knows the right way to build wealth with the minimum of risks; however, high-risk speculation and guessing the unknowable make Wall Street more money than market participants investing to get rich and stay rich. While it may be self-serving to Wall Street, the fact is most market participants like the fun of speculating and willingly participate. Nevertheless, this chasing of greed and guessing about an unknowable future by speculators is good for you, an investor. Why? Because wherever you find greed, fear is also present (**Rule 6**). When greed controls the investment markets, investors watch and enjoy the gains in their portfolio. When the emotions turn and fear grips the speculators and markets, investors are ready to add to their portfolio at fair prices that will boost their annual investment income. It also gives them the potential for capital appreciation as the economy and government-created inflation raise the intrinsic value of their portfolio investments.

Getting rich is a byproduct of inheritance, marriage, hard work, and a bit of luck. Staying rich is another issue. If you see investments as expendable items that change in value almost daily, it will lead you to believe you must take some action regularly to seek more of the same through buying and selling the investments you have, trying to capture price movement of new, more attractive ideas. This is the wrong perspective. What you need to do is think of all your investments, real estate (including your primary residence), fixed-income securities, and common stocks as one all-encompassing business.

When you think of your residence, think of it as the headquarters of your company. When you think of your fixed-income securities, picture them for what they are: loans made to some entity (US government, state or local governments, or corporations). The common stocks in your portfolio are real businesses. Your mindset should be the same as if you had bought the entire company. As your business, your entire portfolio should give you two rewards: cash flow for operating and growing the business, and potential capital appreciation. In effect, you will be building your own multifaceted business, headquartered in your home. As you develop this personal holding company, you will begin to see how one subsidiary (stock in the portfolio) of your company will be improving and growing during part of the economic cycle while another subsidiary may be languishing, with the potential to improve as the economic cycle changes. You will understand that the price you pay for new subsidiaries is crucial to making money over the long term, the same way quality management of your subsidiaries is important.

The financial path to getting rich and staying rich developed in this book, along with the total return portfolio strategy, is designed to assist you in turning the challenging times most people experience into opportunities for improving your future net worth growth. This goal is achieved in three ways:

1. Showing you how to painlessly pay yourself first for being smart.

2. Showing you how to build your portfolio so that at retirement you will not have to worry about outliving your money.

3. Showing you how to add companies to your portfolio at fair prices based on the current value of

companies you are buying, not make some pie-in-the-sky valuation that is based on hopes and prayers, which are guesses about the unknowable future.

Investing is not a game, though Wall Street wants people to think it is. Observers say investing is complicated. That is not true, as shown in **Rule 5.** Speculating is complicated, and Wall Street makes it more so. Wall Street professionals and their marketing machines tell young people to take foolish risks looking for huge rewards because they have a lifetime to make up any losses. That advice not only is nonsensical but borders on irresponsible since Wall Street professionals espousing high unnecessary investment risk-taking know the secret of successful investing, as shown in **Rule 7**.

Investing correctly does not take large amounts of time, but you do have to pay attention. There are only short periods when investors need to be preparing to participate in the markets. You will enjoy the spare time doing other activities while you wait for the investment markets to signal it is time to invest. Smart investing does not take large sums of money to progress on the path to getting rich and staying rich. If you decide to follow these nineteen simple rules, you will benefit and thrive.

Keep this book close by your desk. Read **Rules 15, 16, 17,** and **18** when you have funds to invest. Follow these basic principles and watch your financial security and independence grow over the years. These simple rules are designed to assist you at every stage of your financial life. When the inevitable economic and financial crises come, you will meet those challenges, not by panicking as most speculators will, but by investing in opportunities to increase your net worth and your portfolio's total return. To get started, it's critical to understand the investment markets' reality so you can avoid mistakes and develop your net worth and portfolio to reflect your and your family's wants and needs.

PART II

INVESTMENT MARKETS' REALITY

The Investment Markets' Reality

The investment markets have always been speculative but have become more so over the past forty years. This is reality, and ironically it is good for investors with discipline and patience. Give thanks for these speculators who are part of Wall Street's trading and guessing games. Speculators' mood swings create opportunities for investors and create potential capital appreciation in investors' portfolios. Taking advantage of speculators' fear and greed is key to getting rich and staying rich. Traders enjoy the games created by Wall Street for encouraging volatility, buying, and selling. Investors choose to stay on the sidelines watching, waiting, and already knowing the price they are willing to pay for the investments they want to own. Investors watch patiently for the speculators to flame out like dying comets when fear envelops them. Wall Street's marketing machine and their friends in the business media promote the short-term perspective, enhancing volatility. Investors take advantage of this excessive market churning. They understand the difference between (1) volatility responding to short-term events highlighted by Wall Street and its media friends and (2) long-term economic volatility that results in corporate intrinsic value increases and stock price changes.

Wall Street and its business media friends have even co-opted the definition of *long-term*. Most of the business media define long-term as one to three years. Wall Street has a different definition: three months to one year. Investors think in terms of ten years or forever. Why the difference? Wall Street's focus on volatility, potential capital gains, and turnover of investments is designed to generate fees and market-making opportunities for its members. To facilitate this trading mentality, the business media have even changed how they report price movement to the public. In the past, if a $37.00 stock went up $0.375, the media would report the stock was up three-eighths of a dollar, seemingly an insignificant price movement. Now, the media report the stock went up 1 percent. What difference does this reporting change make? Plenty, because it appeals to the greed emotion in traders.

With no commissions to pay and the ease of borrowing money (margin debt), speculators, focused on generating returns from short-term price movement, will trade to make 1 percent in one day even though the risks far outweigh the potential rewards. This siren song of guessing daily volatility does not entice investors. Investors are looking for total returns that are multiples of their original investments, not percentages. One factor in achieving extraordinary gains is understanding the difference between greed-driven short-term psychological price gains and long-term, economic increases in a company's intrinsic value derived from operations over time, which move the stock price higher.

Over the last forty years, Wall Street firms have carefully and steadily corralled individual investors into their packaged securities, giving the sponsor firms of these mutual funds (MFs) and exchange-traded funds (ETFs) ongoing fees. While some hedge funds, institutional investors, and retail speculators use these premade securities because they are convenient, investors avoid these packaged funds.

Most MFs and ETFs are not conducive to the total return strategy. These funds are the securities many speculators use to try to capture short-term market volatility. There is nothing wrong with that approach for a speculator, but MFs and ETFs raise the unnecessary investment risks higher than is appropriate for investors. Traders are interested only in price movement, not in what the underlying businesses do. Individual speculators have believed the Wall Street marketing message that these managed funds, containing individual securities, will lead them to Wall Street's path to riches just as owning selected individual securities not in a fund package. Unlikely. Some MFs use compounding of returns (if taxes are paid out of other money rather than the MF) and low turnover, but most don't. Funds focus more on capital appreciation than on a total return strategy. Why? Many reasons. We'll discuss seven of them.

First, as one famous mutual fund czar said on a business media program, his fund managers are not wealth managers; they are equity investors. What he meant was their funds' charters require them to invest the dollars sent to them when the money arrives. Since emotions drive the investment markets' pendulum, the money flows in when everyone is greedy, forcing the fund managers to buy stocks while prices are high. Conversely, when fear is rampant and fund shareholders are fleeing, fund managers must sell securities at low prices to meet the withdrawals. Flow of funds, based on the wrong emotions at the wrong time, forces MFs and ETFs to buy high and sell low, just the opposite of what it takes to make money and keep it.

Second, there are other issues that speculators in MFs and ETFs are not aware of or should consider. Funds misapply the concept of diversification. Sector and index ETFs are infamous for touting that their sector funds buy all the stocks in the sector, thus eliminating individual stock risk. That's correct, but it also eliminates single-stock reward. These ETFs use their shareholders' money to buy poorly managed companies along with the well-managed enterprises in the sector or index. They introduce poorly run companies to the portfolio. How many investors want to buy second-rate companies with their hard-earned money? Actively managed ETFs shield their shareholders from knowing what securities are in a portfolio until the end of a specified period. Is this investing? No. It is not only speculating in the stock market but speculating on the skills of the manager.

Third, more than anything else, MFs and ETFs are in a performance contest with their peers to attract speculators' dollars. The latest quarterly performance rankings between competing funds fuels that competition. The winner of the Highest Quarter-by-Quarter Return Contest is determined by the funds' performance compared to some market index benchmark, but not compared to the long-term goal of the fund's shareholders. Wall Street heightens this peer rivalry each quarter by highlighting the funds that performed the best in the prior quarter. In a quarterly performance contest, there is no place for an investment that may take years to develop and eventually grow to be five to ten times the initial investment. Most MF and ETF managers can't be patient and wait for the huge payoff in a few years since the funds' results are publicized in this quarter-to-quarter contest, and their shareholders, not understanding the assets in the funds' portfolios, are always looking to switch to a better-performing fund.

Fourth, when a handful of stocks dominate a market, which usually happens as a rising market continues for years, many of the MFs and ETFs find a way to own those high-flying companies no matter what investment style the fund professes.

Fifth, most fund bylaws prohibit them from using old-fashioned leverage, defined as borrowing money to buy individual stocks. In the investment markets today, Wall Street has created securities, such as options, futures, and swaps, that can introduce leverage to a portfolio without the traditional borrowing of dollars. Some funds may use these specially designed securities, all of which introduce leverage into their portfolios, to amplify returns—either positive or negative. The unnecessary investment risks are higher than many investors understand.

Two documents contain the types of risks (including nontraditional leverage) that are permissible in MFs and ETFs: the funds' *prospectus* and *additional information* literature. These documents must list the risks and strategy inherent in the fund. Anyone thinking of putting money into a MF or ETF should read both documents from at least two different fund sponsors. After reading these documents, an investor will question why they should own a MF or ETF and take the additional risks associated with funds rather than owning a portfolio containing individual securities that they selected based on their unique portfolio objectives of getting rich and staying rich.

Sixth, in the social world today, when some activists believe their perspective is the only one that matters, fund sponsors find themselves pressured by activists, politicians, and some fund holders to adopt a stance reflecting the activists' narrow viewpoint. Investment decisions based on social issues have a high probability of causing the funds' beneficial shareholders to own securities based on these social determinants rather than on financial factors, stifling the opportunity for these funds' beneficial holders to make money.

Seventh, over the years, most fund managers have failed to consistently beat the market indices, which, in the past, was considered a mediocre performance. Fund managers and institutional investors developed the belief that if they replicated a specific index's performance, their jobs would not be at risk due to falling behind the index and their peers' performance. Wall Street's marketing machine has focused on the low-cost aspect of some funds to divert shareholders' attention from the mediocre long-term performance of these funds.

Professional, pseudo-professional, and individual participants in the investment markets have embraced technology, leading to greater trading volume and volatility. Computer screens, algorithms, and high-speed communication capabilities have merged to capture small price movement in such frequency that traders and market-makers gain and lose millions of dollars every day. If the markets are trending, many algorithms offer the user a tool for decision-making. If the markets experience high volatility or an extended or sharp decline, while some computer-driven strategies will shift from positive to negative, many computer programs are likely to be whipsawed by the change in volatility before adjusting to the market's change of direction. Speculators in their funds usually suffer the consequences. Quantitative algorithm speculating has the potential to enhance volatility, which investors can use to their advantage.

In both the packaged securities and recommendations of individual securities, Wall Street sets up simple categories for segmenting companies into types: "growth" stocks and "value" stocks. At various points in either the economic cycle or the investment cycle, the Wall Street marketing machine highlights and recommends one type of stock over another. This rotation from one group to another enhances market volatility and fees paid but does not enhance the bedrock requirement for getting rich and staying rich.

Wall Street's idea of a growth stock is one that experiences (or hopes to experience) a rapid rate of revenue growth. The company may or may not have earnings. Growth stocks usually do not pay a dividend, or if they do later in their life cycle, it's a small percentage of their stock price. These companies are the leaders of any bull market. As the stocks are pushed higher and further away from their current intrinsic value, Wall Street finds reasons to justify an even higher stock price.

Wall Street's definition of a value stock is a company with a mature business model in a mature economic sector where any revenue or earnings growth will be either small or cyclical, depending on economic conditions. These companies' stock prices are usually closer to their current intrinsic value and their dividend percentage relative to their stock price is usually above the overall market dividend yield. Wall Street's attitude is these companies trade at lower valuations than growth stocks. They speak about "value" traps.

In valuing companies, Wall Street uses various methodologies. The two dominant ones are (1) the discounted cash flow (DCF) model and (2) the dividend discount model (DDM). Both methods require the user to make guesses about future factors that are unknowable. For instance, in the DCF, guessing a company's future cash flows for a certain number of years is necessary. How many years? Some analysts use five years, others seven, still others ten. It's not logical or possible to know future cash flows without knowing these unknowable factors:

the state of the economy each year

the level of competition

the level of interest rates

the level of inflation

the weather during the years selected

The resulting yearly cash flow numbers must be discounted back to the present. What discount rate should be used? Inflation plus a real rate of return? What will inflation be over the period? The ten-year US Treasury yield? Certainly, the analysts can ask the company's management for their estimates, but management has the same handicap: it's not possible to know each of the inputs for each of the years selected. Get one or more of the inputs wrong, and the investment can turn into a major loss, even if the company grows over time. Why? Because the initial stock price paid was too high.

The DDM is different but still requires guesses of unknowable information. Using this method, the analyst determines whether the present dividend will be paid for an extended time and whether the dividend will grow in the future. Both guesses are subject to future unknowable circumstances. Depending on who is calculating the DDM, the company's cost of equity (or weighted average cost of capital) must be calculated. This is doable for the current period, but what about the future? If interest rates change, will the required company's capital cost change? What about inflation? Some DDM users substitute the investors' required rate of return instead of capital costs. Similar guesses for the rate of return are necessary. The dividend growth rate is crucial to get correct, yet it is also unknowable. Remember, dividends are declared by the company's board of directors and are not guaranteed.

Guessing the future, either cash flows or dividend payments, is the basis of much of what Wall Street does and recommends. Guessing is not a stable way for you to get rich and stay rich. No one knows the future, but we do know the present. There are methods to determine a fair price to pay for a company's current operations and intrinsic value. One is discussed and developed in **Rule 18**. Focusing on the relationship between the company's current intrinsic value and the stock price is the beginning. A business's fundamental value and its changes over the preceding five years can help you judge the company's management quality and their ability to meet whatever the future brings.

$

PART III

INVESTMENT STRATEGY
AND
RULES 1 THRU 9

Total Return Strategy

You want your portfolio to reflect your own hopes, aspirations, and risk tolerance and your family's unique circumstances. You want to own companies you believe will appreciate over time and pay you income as they grow. Why? Because in times of high market stress and financial crisis, you won't panic since you chose the companies in your portfolio and know these businesses have weathered financial crises and market declines in the past. You know the relationship between the price paid for a company's shares and the company's current operational value. Further, you will receive and reinvest the investment income generated by your portfolio, even when the portfolio's asset values decline as fear grips the markets or sectors. How is this possible? By using a **total return strategy,** putting equal weight on steady investment income from dividends and interest as well as potential capital appreciation. There is another benefit: using the total return strategy, the investment income and fixed-income assets in an investor's portfolio will modify the portfolio's total decline when the markets are under stress.

There may come a time when your career and other activities, as well as the size of your portfolio, cause you to want a professional investment manager. Paying a fee to an SEC-registered investment advisor (RIA) who crafts a portfolio to reflect your unique situation makes sense. Using your brokerage financial consultant to help find the right manager is the place to start. Explain to your contact you want a manager who is willing to take your goals and desired strategy and work with you to construct a total return portfolio strategy using individual securities. This personalized attention is crucial. While many RIAs want their clients to fit into their firm's strategy model, there are managers who have the knowledge and experience to craft portfolios unique to each client.

The most important aspect of the relationship with an RIA is your communication with the manager. You have a responsibility to communicate clearly with a manager, helping them understand your expectations and desires.

Not only should you be able to explain your desires and expectations, but you should also give the RIA a written copy of the portfolio parameters you want. The manager should communicate how their skills and experience will accomplish your goals within your guidelines. The right RIA, capable of constructing a unique portfolio to assist you in meeting your goals the way you want, is worth whatever fee they charge. Think of your relationship with the RIA this way: You are the CEO of the portfolio. You set (1) the criteria of using only individual securities, (2) the target annual portfolio investment income percentage, (3) the target asset allocation between fixed-income securities and common stocks, and (4) the level of diversification between economic sectors. The manager is the chief operating officer, implementing the investment plan to meet the goals within the guidelines.

Make no mistake, investors delight in the speculative volatility from greed because their portfolio companies participate in the stock market's upward momentum. Using the total return strategy, the investors' portfolios also generate annual income higher than the market's annual dividends, and, over time, many of the stocks appreciate by multiples of their cost basis even as portfolio companies increase profits, which can lead to increased dividends. Why? Because the stocks in the portfolio were selected at fair prices reflecting a reasonable relationship between the companies' current intrinsic value and the stock prices. As the businesses continue to operate and current intrinsic value increases, share prices increase. Investors use the portfolio's fixed-income securities to boost annual investment income, which, in times of stock market stress, generates stable income and are available for investing in new opportunities at fair prices.

Getting rich and staying rich require clear thinking about a family's total net worth and needs. Cash reserves, real estate, fixed-income securities, and common stocks all come together in a combination to make you wealthy beyond what you ever expected. Nineteen simple and effective rules make wealth happen. Here's how you do it.

Rule 1: Know Yourself and Your Goals

Stop right here. If you are a person who enjoys daily investment market volatility and the idea of buying stocks or fixed-income assets today and selling them next week for a profit, and you like the excitement of watching the analysts on television or being in chat rooms on the internet, don't read any further. The total return strategy and the other rules are not for you. Consider going out and find a second job, because you may eventually need it. But if you just want to accumulate a net worth that will give you the luxuries in life you desire and the peace of mind of never having to rely on others for your financial well-being, this book will show you how to achieve your goals. Read on.

— RULE 1 —

You must have:
- discipline
- patience
- and know your goals

Why does Rule 1 begin by telling you to stop reading? Investing takes patience, discipline, and knowledge of your goals. Not everyone has those three traits. Even so, every investor is part speculator, but not every speculator is part investor. The gambling mentality in the investment markets appeals to the speculative greed in everyone. It's fun to speculate. The question is this: Can you control your greed, channeling this emotion into a strategy that will make you money over your lifetime? Can you maintain the principles contained in these rules that are contrary to what most speculators are doing? It's necessary to understand that periods of the market's greatest greed will cause you to doubt your strategy, but you must stick with the rules. If you do, your portfolio will grow over the long term, more than you thought possible. At times, other investment strategies will appear to generate more and faster capital appreciation. At other times, your success over the long term will confirm that the total return strategy using these rules is superior to other strategies. The longer you follow the nineteen rules, the more you will understand and trust this path to sustainable wealth.

Decide what investing goals are right for you. Prioritize your goals: stability of the family's finances, your children's education, travel, a financially secure retirement, or whatever is important to you. Keep these goals in front of you. Don't worry about how much you have for investing; a successful investing strategy starts slowly with a small amount and steadily builds momentum. Keep your grip on discipline and patience.

Rule 2: Understand That No One Knows the Future

Wall Street's guessing the unknowable is based on predicting the future performance of the global and US economies and of individual companies. The problem is that no one can predict the future—not what will happen next week, next month, next quarter, next year, or any time beyond that. Why? Because the future is unknowable. Why? Decisions and events impacting the outcome of an event in the future take place in the future. It's important to understand that. Even when analysts develop a range of possible outcomes for revenue and earnings, the range and plot points are just guesses that can be devastating to your investments if wrong. Yet much of Wall Street's research is based on implying that the future economic environment is knowable.

Further, the analysts rely on corporate management to give them a likely range of projected earnings. They build elaborate models, but the inputs into the model are unknowable guesses, not facts. The future is discounted back to the present day using current discount interest rates, which may not be accurate for the entire period being projected. So, inaccurate earning guesses for years into the future are discounted back by unknowable discounting interest rates for each year of the projection. Calmly thinking about this guessing game brings its illogical aspect to the forefront.

— RULE 2 —

Understand that no one
knows the future.

In the fall of 2019, who but the Chinese Communist Party leadership knew COVID-19 would spread around the world, disrupting lives and economies and killing millions? Who knows what economic and tax policies will come out of Washington in the future? Who knows what natural disasters will strike in critical geographic areas, causing economic disruption and stock market volatility next month or next year? Who knows what financial engineering or loose regulations will lead to excessive leverage and speculation, followed by a deleveraging implosion? No one knows, yet Wall Street is full of pundits, analysts, and money managers with the hubris to believe they can see the future. If no one can know the future, how can investors find good long-term securities to add to their portfolios? Here's how.

Understanding the estimated current intrinsic value of a company and gauging the marketplace's current attitude toward the economic sector and individual company will assist in finding a fair valuation for a company's stock. And that is what you, the investor, want: to own parts of successful companies, with competent and confident management, at a fair price for their current business. Let me repeat: as an investor, you want to buy a successfully operating company based on its current operations (revenue and earnings), not on what may or may not happen in the future. This perspective is heresy on Wall Street. Leave the unknowable guesses to Wall Street and its speculator followers, since their games are what eventually give you the opportunity to increase your investment income and potential capital gains.

Rule 3: Success Is NOT Selling Assets in Retirement

Wall Street loves the concept it has fostered that promotes a person or family in retirement selling some of their assets each year for living expenses. It suggests you should have to guess how long you will live and worry about whether you have enough assets to survive throughout your life. Wall Street has even developed mathematical calculations to dazzle clients. It calls these programs "Monte Carlo Simulations." The client must guess the following factors:

- How much money will be available at retirement?
- How much their living expenses will be at the beginning of retirement?
- How high the inflation rate will be during retirement?

- How much the annual return on their portfolio will be before and during retirement?

These four guesses are totally unknowable at any point in time but getting any one of the four wrong can lead to significant challenges long into retirement. Why even bother with the exercise? By the way, there are two other critical guesses not discussed in a Monte Carlo exercise:

- The possibility of a family situation that requires a sizable withdrawal from the portfolio during retirement, over and above regular withdrawals for living expenses.
- The economic and financial environment, stock market level, and interest rates if or when a family emergency happens.

Stop and think: Can you imagine the daily stress of worrying about outliving your assets? Can you imagine, in your late seventies or eighties, watching the stock market drop 40 percent or watching the monetary authorities manipulate and suppress fixed-income interest rates below market rates as they did from 2008 through 2022, even as they developed policies to raise inflation to unacceptable levels? Using a strategy in which a family must spend a portion of their assets each year is unsuccessful wealth building and is not acceptable or necessary for investors.

Finally, look back in history: investment cycles last for six to twelve years. When a cycle turns, the stock market may drop 30 to 90 percent for a period lasting eighteen to thirty months. You should plan for a severe market decline through the structure of the portfolio, which the total return strategy and these nineteen rules do.

— RULE 3 —

Success is NOT having to sell
assets in retirement.

Investors who build portfolios during their asset accumulation years with a total return objective give equal weight to the amount of annual income the portfolio generates from dividends, interest, and potential capital gains. Using this strategy builds income from dividends and interest steadily over the years of accumulating assets. At retirement or when a need arises, the investment income will replace most, if not all, of your earned income that is missing in retirement. These nineteen rules and total return investment strategy minimize market volatility's impact on portfolio flexibility. Guesses about your longevity are no longer determinants of retirement financial security. Isn't knowing better than guessing?

Rule 4: Correctly Prioritize Your Wealth Accumulation Strategy

You should focus on only four asset classes: cash reserves, fixed income securities, common stocks, and real estate. It is crucial you understand this simple fact and build your portfolio the right way from the beginning. Why? These are the asset classes in which you can choose individual investments that fit your needs without paying someone ongoing fees to create a package that contains investments that you don't want or that could cause your portfolio to underperform. In addition, these are the four asset classes that give you the opportunity for both current income and potential capital gains without artificial timelines or early redemptions.

— RULE 4 —

Prioritize building your asset accumulation correctly:
1. Establish 6 months of living expense cash reserves.
2. Own your home with a 30-year fixed-rate mortgage.
3. Own individual fixed-income securities.
4. Own individual common stocks.

The absolute first step in becoming rich and staying rich is to develop a cash reserve away from the investment portfolio. Put aside the amount you need to maintain your after taxes and deductions living expenses for six months. **Rule 14** details how to build and maintain these critical cash reserves. When your lifestyle expenses increase, make sure the amount in this cash reserve increases proportionally. Do not worry about the earnings from these assets. Your only concern is access to these assets if your regular income stops or you have an emergency.

The next priority asset class is real estate. Your primary residence should be the first real estate you buy. **Rule 16** covers this strategy in detail. Just know the important goal is to stabilize your cost of housing for as long as possible.

The third and fourth asset classes are developed together. Think of the third asset class, fixed-income investments, as loans made to multiple entities such as businesses or governments. These are securities in which a fixed amount of interest or dividends is paid annually to you and, at a specific date in the future, the initial investment is returned. **Rule 17** gives the right information to build a fixed-income strategy for any economic environment, even one in which the monetary authorities suppress interest rates. Fixed-income securities have three functions in the portfolio: (1) they supply steady cash flow, (2) they modify the portfolio's volatility, and (3) in times of severe stress on common stock values, they are available for selling and reinvesting the proceeds in common stock opportunities.

The fourth asset class is common stocks of quality companies. In the stock market, the global and US economies fit into eleven macroeconomic sectors. This is important to know and unnecessary to worry about. Make sure your brokerage custodian has a research department that gives you online access. If the firm doesn't, you are using the wrong broker or custodian. Their research department will indicate what macroeconomic sector a particular company is in. **Rule 18** covers the best strategy for common stock investing.

No matter what any Wall Street marketing person tells you, these are the only four asset classes you want to

invest in. Cash reserves, fixed-income securities, common stocks, and real estate will give you the potential to get rich and stay rich. Gold, silver, art, commodities, options, swaps, futures, and cryptocurrencies are all speculative ways to separate you from your money. All of these assets are part of the Wall Street game of guessing the unknowable future. You, as an investor, are looking to own pieces of good businesses bought at a fair price and operated by management confident enough to reward you, the business owner, with a portion of the earnings in the form of dividends each year. As with all gambling and speculating, the traders using the Wall Street–created packaged securities may win now and then, but the market-making firms are the winners in the end. By focusing on the basic four asset classes and adhering to these nineteen rules, you will build a net worth that will give you the opportunity for financial freedom, luxury, stability, and security.

Rule 5: Investing Is Not Complicated; Get Over Your Fear

Wall Street and its marketing teams have built an aura around investing that confuses and intimidates even some professionals, much less the individual investor. Wall Street deliberately blurs the line between speculating and gambling, both of which are complex, and investing. Their purpose appears to be moving individuals toward speculating rather than investing. It's a smoke screen. Investing is simple. Seven single-syllable words tell you what to do to be successful: **buy low and hold for ten years.** Not hard to understand. The complexity arises when you focus on speculating and trying to guess the future. These nineteen rules will help you understand what a fair price is for an investment so you will be buying "low."

Why hold for ten years? Stories abound about large returns accruing to private equity and venture capital investors. A major portion of these gains comes from these investors accepting illiquidity and leverage risks, meaning they are unable to sell their investments for seven to ten years or longer and borrow money to increase the potential gains. Investing in public companies at a fair price and holding for ten years has the potential to reward patient investors with similar above-average capital gains and investment income with lower risks than these private equity and venture capital investors accept. The fact is significant capital appreciation takes time. Should an investor sell a company bought at the right price after ten years? **Rule 18** answers that question. Remember, even investors experience speculative greed and fear, just like aggressive speculators. Control of those emotions comes from the discipline and patience created by having and understanding an investment strategy that works.

Get over any fear of losing money. All market participants, no matter their skill level or experience, will make mistakes in selecting investments. The prices of some securities will fall after you buy them. The unknown future will sometimes cause seemingly correct decisions today to look bad later. Using the principles discussed in these rules

— RULE 5 —

Don't be afraid of investing; it's simple.
Buy at a fair price and hold for 10 years.

may reduce the number and severity of any selection or timing mistakes. The built-in annual cash flow component of the total return strategy will further lessen any portfolio impact from volatility. Many timing mistakes are temporary setbacks as a stock price already under selling pressure declines more in the short term, only to recover over time and rise above the initial investment price later. The successes you will experience with these rules will outweigh any permanent capital losses.

Rule 6: Understand the Investment Pricing Pendulum

Every investment has a price at which it is attractive. Finding the price range encompassing the attractive price is the goal. The discovery begins by understanding every price has two components: *current intrinsic value of the asset and the market's attitude about that intrinsic value.* It's possible to use this method to value any potential investment in the four important asset groups. Stock price volatility usually results from speculators' and investors' attitude about the future intrinsic value, which is different from current intrinsic value and requires guesses about the future.

Study the above Investment Pricing Pendulum. Let's deconstruct its components. Consider the center pole

holding up the pendulum to be the current intrinsic value of the investment. As the center, it's where current fear and greed for the investment are balanced. The words fear and greed are at the bottom of the pendulum base, representing the emotions of the marketplace in respect to the investment, and on the pendulum's top bar, representing the emotion you should have, based on the location of the pendulum ball over the bottom bar.

— RULE 6 —

When the market is greedy, be fearful.
When the market is fearful, be greedy.

Notice the words *fear* and *greed* are more pronounced the farther they are from the pendulum's center pole. The shading of these words represents the intensity of the market's emotions as the investment moves further away from its current intrinsic value. Notice the pendulum itself has a dollar sign and pointed end at the top, which moves in the opposite direction from the actual pendulum ball. This upper point documents the potential reward for the investor from an investment as the pendulum ball swings. The pendulum assists in understanding the market's attitude toward an investment at any time and the fact an investor's attitude should be the opposite.

If the center pendulum pole represents current intrinsic value, how do you determine intrinsic value? It's a different calculation for each asset class. See **Rules 16**, **17**, and **18**.

Rule 7: Understand the Importance of Annual Cash Flow and Compounding Returns

Getting rich and staying rich require consistent and steady portfolio development over time, using the two key factors available to every investor and speculator: steady cash flow and compounding returns. The problem is most market participants either don't know these critical factors or ignore them in the greedy pursuit of outsized short-term gains. Let's look at both factors, which are so crucial to wealth accumulation.

We'll start with the power of steady cash flow coming into the portfolio. Focusing on equal objectives of potential capital appreciation and steady cash flow from dividends and interest is a total return strategy (**Rule 15**). Why is steady cash flow important? First, the investment markets usually give at least two opportunities a year to add a good business to your portfolio at fair prices. The steady cash flow from dividends, interest, and your regular contributions will allow you to seize these opportunities without having to sell other securities. The longer the portfolio is in place, and the longer securities in the portfolio are allowed to remain, the more investment cash flow will grow and be available for deployment at the right time. As an aside, there is another benefit to an equal focus on investment income and potential capital appreciation. Following these nineteen rules, the closer you are to retirement, the more your portfolio investment income will approach the income you have from work. You will have flexibility in determining when you want to give up work income and use the portfolio income in retirement. Finally, economic cycles are such that the monetary authorities may deliberately suppress interest rates while the stock market is under intense price pressure from a faltering economy or a financial crisis. The portfolio investment income and your contributions will put you in the enviable position of having liquid assets to deploy when most investors and speculators don't.

— RULE 7 —

Focus on steady cash flow and
compounding returns.

Growth speculators who ignore dividends in favor of rapid growth say they will sell some shares of a current investment to buy a new opportunity. Really? How does that make sense? If the stock market or economy is moving higher, why sell a stock that is participating in the surge? If the stock market is under selling pressure because of either economic issues or a financial crisis, why sell a stock that may have temporarily given back a large portion of its previous gains or may not have had time to increase its intrinsic value?

In the short term, when the stock market is surging higher, a portfolio of rapidly growing companies that do not pay dividends will outpace a portfolio of companies growing slower and sharing the profits with their shareholders through dividends. Over time, however, the dividends will accumulate and be reinvested in other companies at fair prices, building the portfolio through compounding.

Even value investors will criticize a total return strategy in favor of their narrow focus on stock price versus fundamentals.

Why? Because a total return strategy does not just look at the stock price in relation to the fundamentals. It seeks companies with businesses that are performing well now, with competent and confident management willing to share the profits with shareowners. There is one undeniable fact that makes the total return strategy best for compounding returns: the steady cash flow into the portfolio from the investments allows you to take advantage of opportunities when they arise while maintaining previous investments for the minimum ten-year period, leading to potential portfolio appreciation.

The second part of the strategy for getting rich and staying rich is structuring your portfolio for less volatility to enhance the compounding of returns over a long period. Reread that last sentence and pay attention to the words *long period.* The longer a portfolio is allowed to compound its returns, the larger the portfolio becomes, and, just as important, the more investment cash flow is generated to supplement potential capital appreciation and join with what you and possibly your employer (for retirement accounts) contribute.

What does compounding mean? Here's an example. You start with $1,000 and you earn 10 percent on your money per year. At the end of the first year, you have $1,100 ($1,000

× 10% = $1,100). At the end of the second year, you have $1,210 ($1,100 × 10% = $1,210). In other words, you earn more income (dividends, interest, or capital appreciation) not only on your original principal but on the prior years' earnings as well.

There is a simple way for you to understand the power of this concept. The Rule of 72 will either show you the average annual investment return (AAIR) necessary for your portfolio to double in value or give you the time period required for your money to double if you know the AAIR. For instance, if a portfolio grows at an AAIR of 9 percent, it will take eight years to double (72 / 9 = 8). If you know a time period, such as six years, you can find the AAIR required to double the portfolio, in this case 12 percent (72 / 6 = 12).

A point about compounding: the portfolio value accelerates the longer the time period. For instance, if a person aged thirty has $50,000 and compounds the portfolio value at 7.2 percent per year, the portfolio will be $100,000 in ten years, $200,000 in twenty years, $400,000 in thirty years, and on and on, doubling the value each ten-year period. See why it is irresponsible for someone to urge a young person to take unnecessarily high risks, just because they have time to recoup losses? Suppose the individual in our example lost $20,000 of their $50,000 in some high-risk investment that failed. Now, their remaining $30,000 will only be $240,000 in thirty years. So, the loss of the $20,000 was actually a $180,000 loss. Wall Street's perspective of time to recoup losses understates the risks to getting rich and staying rich. Time is more important than they admit.

It does take time to reap the best rewards from compounding returns. You can control how long you stick with the strategy, but for a given AAIR, the time factor is set. What you can do to grow the portfolio faster, using the two factors of steady cash flow and compounding returns, is to enhance the AAIR by making it an average annual total change (AATC). How do you do that? By taking advantage of any employer contribution to your retirement account and making regular contributions to your portfolio by following the suggestions in **Rule 9.** For example, suppose your portfolio AAIR is 9 percent. If you choose to add 1.5 percent of your portfolio value through your contributions each year, including any employer match in your retirement account, the AATC becomes 10.5 percent, and instead of doubling every eight years, the portfolio will double in 6.8 years (72 / 10.5 = 6.8 years).

Placing your assets in the correct accounts to minimize current and future taxes and making regular contributions from your other income without reducing your current and future lifestyles are key. These two measures combine to enhance the compounding of your wealth.

Of the three components of AATC—potential capital appreciation, investment income, and your contributions—the steadiness of investment income and your contributions keeps the portfolio flexible so you can seize any opportunities that come along each year, increasing further potential capital appreciation and investment income.

You are the determinator of the AAIR and AATC of your portfolio. Being able to take advantage of opportunities the markets present every year is critical. Doing so enhances your probabilities of getting rich and staying rich. Aren't those the goals?

Rule 8: Improve Your Compounding AAIR and AATC by Selecting the Right Accounts

Beyond taking advantage of AAIR and AATC, you can enhance them. This is how to get started. Step one is to open brokerage accounts at a reputable broker. Which one? Two criteria: (1) the firm has a physical office in a city close by, and (2) it has a quality and comprehensive research department available to clients through online access. Open the account in person with a financial consultant in the nearby office who can be called upon when necessary. Online access to trading and research is what is important; however, there are times it's crucial to talk in person with someone who is knowledgeable and has access to the firm's operational personnel.

When you arrive, have written investment objectives and a strategy (See Appendix B) to give to the investment professional. Easy communication is important. Understand the way the brokerage firm works. Ask questions. Feel comfortable with the answers. Investment advice is not important; having the representative's help when necessary is important. Open a taxable account with check-writing privileges and at least one retirement account. Decline a debit card, but accept checks for the taxable account. Specifically tell the professional the account should not have a margin feature. This last request about margin capabilities is important. At this point, you should have an employer retirement account, your own retirement accounts, and a taxable account.

Later, take time to explore the firm's research department's online services. It won't take long. Few facts and figures are needed, but it is helpful to get the information in one place. With the accounts open, it's time to understand how to construct a tax-efficient portfolio.

No one likes to pay taxes. Taxes, however, are a fact of life, so it is important to minimize taxes in both the short and long terms, so the portfolio value compounds the fastest. There are three types of accounts for accumulating fixed-income and common stock assets:

— RULE 8 —

To minimize total taxes and improve compounding, place investments in these accounts:

Tax-Deferred Account
- Fixed-income assets with the highest interest and dividends.
- Corporate preferred stocks with long maturities.

Tax-Free Account
- Common stocks with high dividends and high potential capital gains.

Taxable Account
- Fixed-income assets with short maturities.
- Common stocks with low or no dividends.
- Special situation common stocks.

1. retirement accounts that allow the account holder to make contributions on a pre-tax basis (traditional IRAs, SEP IRAs, 401k, 403b, 457)

2. retirement accounts that allow the account holder to make contributions on an after-tax basis (Roth accounts)

3. completely taxable accounts without any special governmental tax preference or restriction

You need to understand a few things about these. First, any accounts with special tax features, such as IRAs and employer-sponsored retirement accounts, are subject to the whims of Congress. The federal government is the biggest debtor in the country. When Congress needs more tax dollars, any special tax exemptions, such as retirement accounts, are subject to Congress changing the rules, which they have done many times over the years.

Second, understand what assets you can and should place in different accounts. Employer-sponsored retirement accounts, either traditional or Roth, such as the 401(k), 403(b), and 457, usually restrict investments to a preselected group of mutual funds. This is not advantageous to you; however, the most important feature of these accounts is the employer-matching contribution. You should take full advantage of the employer-matching deposits. If your employer does not match your contributions and restricts investments to MFs and ETFs, funding your own self-directed retirement account is better. Individual IRAs, both traditional and Roth, and SEP IRAs are available for those who know individual securities make sense for their personal financial strategy. It is important to understand your investment options with your employer retirement plan and to know whether your employer contributes to the account.

Traditional retirement accounts have the special advantage of tax deferral on any income and realized capital gains until the assets or sales proceeds leave the accounts. Notice the word *deferral*. You must eventually pay the taxes on all of these assets and earnings when they are taken from the account. The IRS will tax every dollar withdrawn at your regular income tax rate in the year of withdrawal, even if the proceeds come from a realized capital gain. The additional taxable income from retirement account withdrawals is added to your other taxable income, pushing you into a higher tax bracket. Further, the retirement account rules force the account holder to start taking withdrawals from tax preference retirement accounts at a certain age, even if they don't want or need the money.

Roth accounts are different. In a Roth account, your contributions are made from income that has already been taxed. Only taxpayers earning below an income cap can contribute to a Roth account. There are other restrictions as well. In certain circumstances, traditional (pretax) retirement accounts can be converted to a Roth account by paying the tax due when the conversion is made. Under current law, all income and capital appreciation in a Roth account are free of any tax while the assets are in the Roth IRA or when they are withdrawn from the account (the account and assets must be open for a set period). If you qualify to make Roth contributions, either to an employer account or to your own Roth account, it is important that you can use individual securities rather than MFs or ETFs.

If an account does not have any special tax privileges, it is commonly called a taxable account, meaning the income and capital gains are subject to taxes when you receive them. No one can restrict the investments you place in the account.

There are different tax profiles for different accounts. The goal is to use the accounts' special tax provisions to minimize both current and future taxes. Here are the four steps of the strategy.

First, in the employer-sponsored accounts where you must use mutual funds, make deposits so you receive the full employer-matching contribution. Place both your deposits and the employer match in either a guaranteed income option or an intermediate (less than seven years), high-quality (investment grade), fixed-income fund. Adjust the average maturity of the fixed-income MF when appropriate as stipulated in **Rule 17**. Why primarily fixed-income funds? Because you can't select the common stocks that meet your unique needs. Using these accounts as part of your fixed-income asset allocation makes sense because you will receive the full employer match contribution and regular income distributions from the MF, with the steady cash flow

———— ◆ ————

sheltered from current income taxes. Reinvest the income in the appropriate fixed-income MF as dictated by **Rule 17**. In your other accounts, where you can use individual securities, you will be able to tailor the potential capital gains so you not only defer current taxes but also build in the potential to have the gains tax free.

Second, in traditional IRA or SEP IRA accounts where you can select individual securities (stocks, bonds, or preferred stocks), place all the longer-term (maturities greater than twenty years) fixed-income securities and the common stocks that pay the highest current dividends. Not only will you defer the current taxes on the interest and dividends you receive, but some of the high dividend paying common stocks may appreciate or increase their dividends in the future.

Third, in a Roth IRA, place the common stocks that have (a) the highest amount of fear according to the investment pendulum, (b) a history of increasing dividends on a regular basis, or (c) companies demonstrating an expanding business over the last five years. Notice the Roth account will have only common stocks.

And finally, in the taxable account (current income taxes paid when income is received and capital gains taxes paid when securities are sold), place the shortest-term fixed-income securities (money market funds, maturities of less than three years), all the common stocks with the lowest dividend yield relative to your cost, and investments considered special situations (see **Rule 18**).

Using this placement strategy, you can control most of your common stock and fixed-income asset selection and shelter most of the current dividends and interest from being taxed now. The potential capital appreciation is shielded from ordinary income taxes until far into the future (traditional retirement accounts) or even permanently (gains in the Roth account).

Rule 9: Invest More without Changing Your Current Lifestyle

Few people like giving up enjoyment now for a better future later. That's just human nature, particularly when your family has worked hard to get to where they are. You can maintain and improve your lifestyle while still building net worth for the future. There are three ways a family receives income and assets:

1. Inheritances
2. Gifts
3. Salary and bonuses

Here's what to do with each of them.

The inheritances go into the investment program. These assets are the family legacy and should continue to do what they did for prior generations—give financial security. Apply your compounding calculation to the amount you receive and see what a difference it will make later.

— RULE 9 —

To accumulate wealth without reducing your lifestyle, add these to your investment portfolio:
- 100% of any inheritance
- 50% of any gift
- 50% of any net raise or bonus

Add the other half of a gift, raise, or bonus to your current living budget. Don't forget to increase your cash reserves to six months of the new living expense total.

Split gifts. Enjoy half now and put half into your investment program.

In the future, take half of any net—after taxes and deductions—salary raises and/or bonuses and put it into the investment program. Set up the transfer from your operating account to your investment account so the amount transfers automatically. Use the other half to boost the family's lifestyle and enjoy now.

Using this method for accumulating wealth, your family will have a more secure financial future and be able to meet your goals in life without making significant sacrifices. Start early in life, and the rewards will be more than imaginable. There are, however, personal lifestyle risks that can derail any wealth accumulation program. Minimizing these lifestyle risks is important.

PART IV

PERSONAL LIFESTYLE RISKS TO ACCUMULATING WEALTH

RULES 10 THRU 13

Rule 10: Personal Risk: Lack of Investing Discipline and Patience

Want to know who is keeping you from being as rich as you want to be? Look in the mirror. Investing is like any worthwhile activity; it must be done correctly. Certain rules are necessary to ensure you arrive in the future without the stress of financial hardship. Here are four disciplines to minimize personal lifestyle risk on the way to getting rich and staying rich.

First, you should set up a systematic way to **pay yourself before paying anyone else**. It's simple to do with the banking technology today. The day after payday, have a specific amount transferred automatically from your regular operating bank account, where salaries are deposited and bills paid, to the investment account. Only record in your checkbook the deposit less the amount being transferred to investments. Start with a small amount so you are comfortable with not having those dollars for spending. After three months, if you feel you can up the amount going to investments, do so. Never put yourself in a bind to the point that you must take assets out of the investment account. Remember, you and your family are the most important people you need to take care of.

Second, over time develop your total portfolio so it generates an average of 3.5 percent of the cost basis in dividends and interest annually. Fixed-income securities should average at least 4.66 percent on their cost. With fixed-income investments, shorter maturities pay lower interest. It will take time, but the idea is to build the fixed-income portfolio, so you have securities maturing every couple of years for the next thirty years. There are periods when the fixed-income opportunities do not offer an appropriate yield. Follow the strategy in **Rule 17**, and over time the portfolio will have cash flow from fixed-income securities that is greater than the 4.66 percent objective.

The common stock part of the portfolio should average at least 3 percent of cost annually from dividends. Not every common stock investment will pay a dividend; however, the mix of companies should average 3 percent. There are instances, even when the stock market is under pressure, when an attractive business either does not pay a dividend or pays one that is less than 3 percent. You can still add these companies to your portfolio using the methods discussed in **Rule 18**.

— RULE 10 —

The greatest risk to getting rich is a lack of investing discipline and patience!

Third, don't fall for the wild, but unknowable, projections of above-normal growth for the favorite stocks of the time. Don't believe unknowable interest rate projections. No one knows what is in the future. In your portfolio, gather quality companies and fixed-income securities for which the investment pendulum clearly shows market fear is high (see **Rule 6**). Let the markets tell you the time is right to invest in opportunities at fair prices.

Fourth, make sure the investment account (not including the six months of cash reserves) is a one-way street. Put money in; do not take money out. Give it time to build and build and build.

Rule 11: Personal Risk: Too Much and Wrong Kinds of Leverage

everage is a fancy word for debt. Governments, companies, and individuals experience financial disasters when they borrow too much money in the wrong way. An investor should borrow money for two purposes:

1. a thirty-year fixed-rate mortgage on a principal home or real estate
2. funding or establishing a business

Adjustable-rate mortgages and fixed-rate mortgages of less than thirty years only turn liquid assets, available for living expenses and investing, into illiquid equity in the principal residence or other asset, exposing the borrower to unnecessary interest rate risks and lender demands for repayment at an inconvenient time.

Even when you're not planning to live in a home for long, a thirty-year fixed-rate mortgage gives you, the borrower, not the lender, all the flexibility and options. Do you know what your circumstances will be five years from now? Fifteen years from now? Thirty years from now? No. No one does. The thirty-year fixed-rate loan's interest rate cannot change, and the monthly payment will become a smaller percentage of your growing monthly income over the years, thus giving you more disposable income to enjoy and split with your investment portfolio. If interest rates drop and make it sensible to refinance, don't cash out equity. Refinance the loan balance with a new thirty-year mortgage again. Your monthly payments will decline, and you will still have financial security in your principal residence through a lower monthly payment.

Never borrow money for an investment other than a home, investment real estate, or business. Never make an investment in which the speculator puts up part of the money now and the rest later. If money is needed later, it usually means the investment is in trouble.

Life should be lived so that bills can be paid in full, including credit cards, each month. Credit cards are a form of revolving credit in which the card holder has a line of credit they can use to smooth out cash flows during a month. The interest rates on credit cards are prohibitively high, so the card balance should be paid off monthly. Now, some logistics. You need brokerage accounts. See **Rule 8** for detailed instructions.

— RULE 11 —

Major risks of getting rich:
- Too much leverage.
- Wrong kind of leverage.

As instructed in **Rule 8**, make sure that when you open an investment account, it is not a margin account. Why? Two reasons. First, borrowing money against your security holdings exposes you to unnecessary risks of the brokerage firm requiring you to put up more money or selling your securities if the stock market or individual securities decline. You could be facing a situation in which your securities are sold at a loss and your equity in the account is wiped out.

Second, with a margin account, even if you do not borrow money through the account, the broker or custodian will have the right to lend the shares in the account to a speculator, who will pay a fee for borrowing the shares; however, the monies paid go to the broker or custodian, not to you.

Some custodians will offer securities lending capabilities to clients who do not have a margin account. Under no circumstances should you enter one of these programs. Securities law prohibits tax-deferred accounts, such as IRAs, from being margin accounts. Some custodians, however, have developed a workaround program for lending tax-deferred securities. Do not enter a securities lending program associated with any retirement account assets.

The securities lending risks in a normal market environment are relatively small; however, in a financial crisis, the risks can be huge and can lead to a permanent loss of capital. By not having a margin account or lending agreement, you are protected from these unnecessary investment risks.

As stated above, the worst borrowing most people can do is using credit card debt. The interest rates are very high, usually over 19 percent. The second worst is going to unregulated fintech companies that advertise easy borrowing. It is easy to borrow—and expensive. Conduct your life so that you can pay off your daily expenses and credit card balances from your net monthly income. Debt from undisciplined spending will stymie your get rich program, putting your stay rich program completely out of reach.

Rule 12: Personal Risk: Uncontrolled Insurance Costs

Most insurance was inexpensive in the past. It's expensive now. It can divert a sizable amount of your disposable income from your current lifestyle and your wealth building, but you need to have enough of the right kind. Understand that there are three types of insurance you must have.

Health insurance. This is expensive. You can take steps to control the expense:

1. Take out a health insurance policy with the highest deductible appropriate for you based on your and your family's medical profile. At the same time, if possible, the policy should qualify you for a health savings account (HSA).

2. Set up the HSA.

3. You will save on insurance premiums because of the higher deductible—place half of the premium savings into the HSA every month.

The other half of the premium savings may cover some of the out-of-pocket expenses resulting from the higher deductible. If possible, fund the HSA to the maximum each year since the contributions are tax deductible, but don't take the money from your investment account. In an HSA, the provider will offer a selection of mutual funds. Select a balanced fund (part fixed-income and part stocks). Allow the HSA balance to build up until or unless some large uninsured expense arises. Medical expenses are a major threat to any wealth-building program. Having some insurance coverage for large, uncontrollable medical issues is critical (cancer, stroke, heart problems, chronic conditions, and joint replacements). Normal yearly health visits to medical professionals are not, and those expenses should be paid from your monthly income.

Property insurance. Depending on where you live, you must pay attention to potential serious damage to your home and other properties. If the basic government flood insurance is available for your area, take it, even if your home is not technically in a flood zone. Flood damage from rising water or even wind-driven water is usually not covered in regular homeowner's insurance. Make sure wind damage is available on your policy. It's likely you need a separate policy for wind. Insure for the appropriate amount to potentially rebuild or repair your home. Ask the insurance company what is the maximum appropriate coverage on your home. Why? If you have less than full coverage, the insurance company may pay you less than the amount of the policy. Underinsured property losses can result in critical family financial destruction.

— RULE 12 —

Important risks of getting rich:
- Too much of the wrong insurance.
- Not enough of the right insurance.

Insurance premiums for cars and other properties (boats, motorcycles, etc.) do not automatically go down as your vehicles or property age and depreciate. Every few years, shop around to find the most appropriate rate for the age of your vehicles. Don't over insure but insure for liability and the estimated depreciated value of your properties.

Life insurance. Life insurance is renting an estate until you build one. You can't afford life insurance that completely replaces the lost lifetime income of the insured person. Think of replacing at least three years of after tax earnings if the insured person dies. This time frame gives the family a bridge to adjust their lifestyle to their new circumstances. Several complicated life insurance policies are offered to the public. Beware of these policies. You want to consider only a simple *whole-life* policy (the most expensive come with savings account provisions, which defeats the purpose of the policy) or a *term* insurance policy that pays only the face amount of the policy, without any savings account attached.

The higher premium of a whole-life policy funds a cash value account. You can borrow the cash value if needed, but you pay interest on what you borrow, and if the insured dies while a loan is outstanding, the loan is subtracted from the insurance proceeds paid to the policy beneficiary. If there is no loan, the longer the whole life policy is in place and premiums are paid, the higher the cash value. When the insured dies, the policy face value is paid to the beneficiary, and the cash value is kept by the insurance company, in effect, paying the beneficiary the money the insured paid into the policy plus policy dividends earned supplemented by a smaller amount paid by the insurance company. Your own total return investment strategy coupled with a term life insurance policy may be more beneficial.

The term insurance policy gives the insured the dollar coverage they want during the time the policy is maintained, with no savings account attached. The premium cost is lower than that of the whole-life policy. There are essentially two term policy premium options. First is a term policy in which the premium goes up every year the policy is in place. This is not an attractive option. Second, some companies offer a fixed premium for the period the policy is in force. This is the policy to obtain. The key is to have life insurance coverage while building your net worth, with a fixed premium during the time you are insured. You should aim to have insurance coverage through age sixty-five. At that age, if you followed these nineteen rules and a total return investment strategy, there won't be a need to rent an estate. You'll have one.

Rule 13: Personal Risk: Not Funding Taxable Accounts

Funding only retirement accounts will usually not get an investor a financial net worth large enough to have a stress-free life before or during retirement, particularly if the retirement accounts are employer-sponsored accounts that have only mutual funds as investment choices. The aims of your investment program are (1) allowing your investments the time to grow in value, and (2) generating increasing investment income so that, at retirement, instead of having to sell assets to replace working income, your portfolio income replaces all or most of your lost salary.

However, life is real. There are times in life when unexpected challenges require meeting them with financial

— RULE 13 —

Critical risk of getting rich:
Not Funding taxable accounts.

assets. If the challenge takes more than your six months of cash reserves, and all you have left are assets in a tax-deferred account, withdrawing those assets may not be tax efficient. Some retirement accounts allow you to borrow a portion of the account balance, which means you pay interest on the loan, besides forgoing the investment income you would have received on the withdrawn assets. Withdrawing assets from tax-deferred accounts will add unnecessary income taxes and possibly a tax penalty every time a withdrawal is made, depending on your age and method of taking the distributions. Therefore, it can add to the cost of the crisis. Having assets in accounts where you can use them in an emergency without additional tax cost is important.

Taxable accounts and Roth IRAs are where you can build steadily increasing income from dividends and interest as well as potential capital gains and assets available for unexpected events, if necessary. Flexibility in controlling taxes will be greatly enhanced by having assets not subject to additional and unnecessary taxes in the future.

———— ◆ ————

As you can see, the four major personal lifestyle risks are clear and can be minimized. You are the driver of your own financial destiny. Here is how to get to your destination.

PART V

GETTING RICH AND STAYING RICH

RULES 14 THRU 19

Rule 14: Build Family Emergency Cash Reserves

Cash reserves should not be considered part of the investment portfolio and are kept separate. **The return *of* these assets is more important than the return *on* these assets.** These reserves are a family's first safety valve in an emergency. Cash reserves should be equal to six months of your operating income after taxes and deductions. This amount will give you time to think through the best way to financially handle a crisis without adding stress by taking on more debt through credit cards or loans.

The only two assets you should use for these cash reserves are short-term: US Treasury notes or bills and FDIC-insured certificates of deposit (CDs) with maturities of one year or less. You can choose to keep a portion of the reserves in actual cash. The decision to do so is predicated on the interest available on FDIC bank deposits, either a savings account or CDs, and US Treasuries. When interest rates are suppressed by the monetary authorities, choosing actual cash makes sense but does require a lockbox or a safe and secure place. The Treasury securities are available through your broker or custodian or directly from the US Treasury through treasurydirect.gov. You can get the CDs from your local bank (preferred source) or your broker or custodian. The treasuries are better than the CDs because (1) the income is exempt from state and local taxes, and (2) in a national financial crisis, the regulators may close the banks for a time. Treasury securities are not likely subject to restrictions because of the size of their market and the large number of institutions and government entities that own them.

— RULE 14 —

Emergency cash reserves:
- 6 months of living expenses.
- 1 year or less FDIC- insured CD *or*
- 1 year or less US Treasury note.

Return *of* cash reserves is more important than return *on* cash reserves.

———— ♦ ————

The worst mistake you can make with cash reserves is to place them in a security offering more interest than the ultra-safe US Treasury securities or CDs. If a security offers a higher interest rate, you can know there is a higher hidden risk. Every other security than FDIC insured bank deposits and US Treasuries carries some higher liquidity or credit risk. If you need to use the cash reserves, it is because you have an emergency or the economy is in a crisis that could cause your income to be reduced or eliminated. Earning a higher rate of interest on these reserves is not the point. Liquidity and safety are. You take enough risks on your other assets.

Cash reserves mean flexibility to handle unexpected events. Not only are they important to your wealth accumulation, but they can lower your stress level during any disruption in your life, allowing you to make decisions calmly.

Rule 15: Build a Sensible Portfolio Strategy

Let's define your portfolio. Your investments include real estate, initially your primary residence, your fixed-income securities, and your common stocks.

Building the wealth accumulation strategy requires coordinating all three asset classes so you don't fall into the trap of having to sell one asset to hold another you can't sell. To this end, it's important to understand the difference between *liquid* assets and *illiquid* assets.

Common stocks and fixed-income assets are liquid assets because they can be sold anytime the markets are open. While the price may not be attractive, the assets can convert into cash easily.

Real estate is an *illiquid* asset. Even if the price is relatively low compared to similar properties, real estate is expensive to sell and takes time to convert to cash. Real estate normally has a certain amount of leverage (mortgage) associated with it. That means the mortgage balance gets paid before the owner receives proceeds when the property sells. In times of distress, the price of the property may drop below or equal the mortgage balance, leaving nothing for the owner if the asset is liquidated. Owning real estate requires timely payment of the mortgage, taxes, insurance, and maintenance. Failure to pay the taxes and mortgage will probably result in losing the property to creditors. Failure to carry insurance could subject you to a catastrophic blow to your net worth.

The most important real estate strategy is finding the right primary home to buy. The criteria are discussed in **Rule 16**.

Part of your strategy is to borrow the largest amount of the purchase price possible using a thirty-year fixed-rate mortgage, which will make the down payment as small as possible. There is a catch. Too small a down payment may cause the lender to demand monthly mortgage insurance or raise the lender's interest rate higher than its lowest thirty-year rate. Avoid these demands. It has been said before and repeated here: your wealth accumulation is enhanced by locking in housing costs to a fixed amount for as long as possible. That's what a thirty-year mortgage does. More on this issue in **Rule 16**.

Next comes building the *liquid* assets. No matter how young or old you are, all portfolio assets, contributions, and investment income (dividends and interest) should be split so that 70 percent are invested in common stocks and 30 percent are invested in fixed-income assets. Using the total return strategy and this disciplined split of assets, contributions, and investment income reinvestment will position your portfolio to take advantage of all economic cycles and financial crises, and to achieve growth and flexibility.

It's a fallacy that you should switch from common stocks to fixed-income assets when retiring or have 100 percent stocks at a younger age. Here's why. An activist monetary authority (the Fed) coupled with political monetary control has set a policy of targeting 2 percent inflation every year. What this means is the purchasing power of the US dollar will be reduced by at least 20 percent every decade. Stock in well-managed companies will assist in overcoming this deliberate depreciation of money's purchasing power. The fixed-income investments, when allowed to trade at a market yield, will partially compensate for expected inflation and will generate steady cash flow to the portfolio. When the economy or the market faces a crisis, fixed-income assets give you money that you can use to buy good businesses at fair prices. There are very few times you should deviate from this 70-30 allocation. Those exceptions are detailed in **Rule 17.**

— RULE 15 —

Portfolio strategy:
- Choose fixed-income assets with a series of maturities and hold them to maturity.
- Choose common stocks in all macroeconomic groups.
- Choose common stocks with an average dividend return of 3% on cost.
- Hold common stocks for a minimum of 10 years.
- Allocate 30% fixed-income and 70% common stocks for your portfolio and contributions.
- Buy your primary residence before any other real estate.

The asset allocation of contributions, investment income, and assets will shift in response to market signals. If market volatility does not change the contribution and investment income allocation between common stocks and fixed-income securities, over time your portfolio will have a higher and higher percentage of common stocks through capital appreciation and higher annual investment income. **This is what you want.** Even though the fixed-income securities will decline as a percentage of the total portfolio, the actual money in fixed-income securities will increase, giving your portfolio flexibility, income, and liquidity that lets you take advantage of market opportunities or life changes. Finally, with a total return strategy, the increasing investment income will allow reinvestment every year into new assets that generate even more investment income and potential capital appreciation. At retirement, annual investment income could be a large component of available cash flow for replacing salaries and bonuses you've given up.

This portfolio strategy is straightforward, but it's more detailed than most investment professionals expect from individual investors. For that reason, when you speak with your brokerage professional the first time or with an SEC-registered RIA, you should give them a written copy of your investment goals, objectives, and strategy. Appendix B has a sample for you to use or modify. Why a written statement? Not every RIA is willing or experienced enough to develop a portfolio unique to each client. Many do not want to use individual securities; they prefer to use MFs and ETFs. It's better for you to find that out before allowing someone to rearrange your portfolio, potentially creating capital gains taxes you must pay and disrupting the compounding returns and income stream.

Rule 16: Build a Logical Real Estate Investment Strategy

The first and most important asset you should own is your principal residence. Why? Housing is a major ongoing lifestyle cost. If you rent, your landlord can raise your rent every time your lease expires. During economic cycles, when more people are entering the workforce, rents for housing usually increase. What you want to do is to fix, for as long as possible, the major part of your housing expense. You can't do much about property taxes, insurance, or maintenance, but you can fix your principal and interest mortgage payments for a long period. Prequalify for a thirty-year fixed-rate mortgage. Along with the down payment amount, the prequalified loan will signal the target home price range you can afford. Look at all options to minimize the down payment; however, always make sure to qualify for the lowest available thirty-year mortgage interest rate without having to pay mortgage insurance.

Once the house price range is established, look around your community to determine the area that has the best schools (even if you have no children) and access to attractive amenities. There will be several neighborhoods for you to choose from, with homes in various price ranges, in the desired section of town. The determining factor is the home price range you qualify for. Find the smallest, oldest, and most-in-need-of-upgrading house in the best neighborhood you can afford in your chosen area. For example, perhaps there are two homes at the same price you are considering. One house may be new and at the top of the neighborhood's price range. The other home, at the same price, may be one of the least expensive houses in its neighborhood. Your best investment is to buy the older home in a neighborhood of higher-priced homes. Why? Because most of the money will go into the land value, and you can renovate the house over time.

There is another plus to the strategy. You will probably remain in the home longer for two reasons: (1) its neighborhood is better than the other home's neighborhood, and

(2) the ongoing renovations will make the home more pleasing and unique to you as you implement your ideas for comfort and utility. One huge wealth destroyer many people succumb to is selling their home and buying another. Every time a home is sold, significant assets are spent on agent commissions, packing, moving, and renovating the new home. Starting off in a better neighborhood with a home that can be customized as the family expands will eliminate the need to move and incur these expenses.

The thirty-year fixed-rate mortgage is crucial to any real estate strategy. Why? When taken out, the loan is calculated as a certain percentage of your income at that time. Over the thirty years, the mortgage payment will remain the same while your income will probably continue to rise, making

— RULE 16 —

Real estate strategy:
- Buy your principal residence as soon as possible.
- Buy the least expensive house in the best neighborhood you can qualify for.
- Obtain a 30-year fixed-rate mortgage with the lowest down payment that doesn't require mortgage insurance.
- Renovate and expand over time rather than moving.

the mortgage payment a progressively lower percentage of your disposable income. This shift gives you more flexibility to enjoy your hard-earned income and, just as important, build your wealth faster.

Many people think they are being smart by making extra mortgage payments each year. That is a mistake. The interest rate on the loan is fixed. Yes, the extra payment will enable the loan to mature in less than thirty years, but you are not earning (saving) at a rate higher than the stated mortgage interest rate. If the same money goes into your investment portfolio and is allocated according to the formula in **Rule 15**, the average annual total return will likely be much greater than the mortgage interest rate, and you'll have more liquid assets earning more income to use for opportunities or address emergencies in the future.

As your family's wealth grows, you may want to add investment real estate or a second home for vacations. The same principles for buying a primary residence apply to buying the additional real estate. Factor in the various costs the same way you did on your principal home. The mortgage, taxes, insurance, and maintenance recur every year. Renting the property may offset some or all of these expenses; however, if the property is a vacation home, the IRS may limit your use of the property while you are offsetting expenses by renting the home to others. Placing a home on an online rental site may make sense. The key is to examine the numbers. Determine the costs. Find out what the average rental income per night is for your location. See how many nights your property must be rented to cover all the out-of-pocket costs.

There are other emotional pluses and minuses that are unique to you. Having the unemotional numbers helps you make the best decision. As in all investment decisions, examine the Investment Pricing Pendulum. Ascertain the pendulum position between fear and greed. For instance, what is the historical price range for similar property in the area? What percentage of the price is attributable to the land under and around the structure? You are assessing the intrinsic value and how much the current demand for property in the area has changed the price dynamics. The land's historical average price over the last five years will give you a comparison to the current land value. The cost of construction for new structures relative to the price attributable to the existing building will give you an idea of how the construction prices have changed. Real estate is a good anchor to your net worth if you make the decision in a disciplined manner.

Rule 17: Build a Simple Fixed-Income Strategy

Every investor needs to have some fixed-income securities, no matter what the level of interest rates or future rate predictions. Even when monetary authorities suppress the true interest rate, building the fixed-income portfolio is important. The strategy you want to use is simple and takes the interest-rate guessing out of developing a fixed-income group of securities. These investments fulfill important functions in the compounding total return strategy. To understand their importance, it's necessary to understand some of their unique features.

Set payout. A fixed-income security pays a stated amount of interest or dividend each year until maturity, when the entity issuing the security will give the investor back the original face (par) value.

Inverse price relationship with interest rates. The price of fixed-income securities will change inversely with the change in market interest rates. If market interest rates increase, the price of an already-issued fixed-income security will decrease. If market interest rates decrease, the price of an already-issued fixed-income security will increase. The magnitude of the change in price depends on the annual amount of interest or dividend the security pays and the time left before maturity. The higher a security's annual income, the smaller its price response to interest rate changes. The shorter a security's maturity, the smaller its price response as well.

Rating based on credit quality. Markets differentiate fixed-income securities according to their credit quality. US Treasury securities have the highest credit rating of AAA. Other securities, such as municipal bonds, corporate bonds, and corporate preferred stocks, have ratings ranging from AAA (safest) to CCC (riskiest). Credit quality ratings can change. There is a price differential between credit ratings. For instance, a AA rated security may have a .35 percent higher yield than a AAA, and an A rated may have a .50 higher yield than AA, and on through the credit ratings with the lower the rating the higher the yield. The differential yields will change as the markets perceive different risks. Only securities rated AAA to BBB are considered investment grade. There is a reason "junk" is the nickname for non-investment-grade fixed-income securities.

Early redemption feature. US Treasuries do not have early redemption features. Most corporate and municipal fixed-income securities have a redemption call date and call price, which means the issuer can give you back your money before the actual maturity date and require you to give them back the security. This provision is a serious risk to consider when developing your fixed-income securities portfolio. Companies usually redeem fixed-income securities before maturity when they can replace them with a security paying a lower interest rate. This always works to the fixed-income investor's detriment. It's critical to know if a security has an early redemption feature.

In a portfolio, the fixed-income securities have several functions. First, they supply annual dividend or interest income to the portfolio. Second, they are the first securities to sell if the investor has an emergency greater than their cash reserves can handle. Third, in the event of a sharp stock market decline, the fixed-income securities with short maturities (less than three years) are a source of funds, along with your contributions and investment income, for buying additional common stocks.

Changes in the allocation of your investment income and contributions between asset classes should take place when the following conditions are present:

During an economic crisis or a financial panic, if the common stock portion of the portfolio falls to 55 percent or less of the total portfolio. All new contributions, dividends, and interest should be applied to common stocks until the asset allocation returns to a 70–30 asset mix. In the unlikely event that the ten-year US Treasury yield is 6.5 percent or higher at the same time, the allocation split should be 50 percent common stocks and 50 percent fixed-income securities.

If the stock market is controlled by greed, pushing prices higher, and the common stocks reach 85 percent of the total portfolio value. New contributions and investment income should shift to 80 percent new fixed-income assets and 20 percent new common stocks until the 70–30 allocation is restored.

If the ten-year US Treasury note is yielding 6.5 percent or more. All new contributions and income generated should go into twenty-five-year or longer maturity US

Treasury bonds if the yield on those longer maturities is higher than the yield on the ten-year note and the common stocks are above 55 percent of the total portfolio. If the common stocks are below that level, place 50 percent in stocks and 50 percent in the long-maturity Treasuries.

A well-designed fixed-income portfolio will include US Treasury securities, corporate bonds, and corporate preferred stocks. These should be individual securities and not any group of securities in a MF or ETF. Why? Besides trying to guess the direction of interest rates, these fund managers must distinguish themselves from their peer competitors. They do this not only by seeking out certain securities barely within credit quality parameters, but also by seeking out securities with low stated dividend or interest rate and as long a maturity as possible in order to introduce more volatility in their portfolio. They then attempt to trade securities for capital appreciation. You, on the other hand, want steady and high cash flow as your objective since you intend to hold the fixed-income securities until they mature.

If the ten-year US Treasury yield is 7 percent or more and corporate preferred stocks yield 8 percent or higher on BBB- rated securities. When the ten-year US Treasury yield is 7 percent or more and corporate preferred stocks yield 8 percent or higher on BBB- rated securities, add the preferred stocks with maturities from forty years to perpetual (no maturity) to your portfolio up to 10 percent of the total fixed-income value. Since the preferred stocks all have redemption call dates, examining the time left before redemption is critical.

Maturities should extend from two years to over thirty years. When you're building your portfolio, maturities of two to five years should be investment grade (AAA to BBB) corporate bonds with some securities maturing every couple of years (don't forget to examine the redemption call feature). Maturities from eight to thirty years should be US Treasury notes and bonds, with some issues maturing every five years.

— RULE 17 —

Fixed-income investment strategy:
- All investment grade (AAA to BBB).
- Series of maturities from 2 to 30+ years.
- Corporate bonds in maturities from 2 to 5 years.
- US Treasuries for maturities from 6 to 30 years.
- Corporate preferred stocks for maturities longer than 30 years.
- Maturity selection based on the US Treasury 10-year note yield.

———◆———

Developing and keeping track of your fixed-income portfolio is easy. Set up an Excel workbook (See Appendix A for complete instructions). Populate the Excel fixed-income sheet as follows. When adding a fixed-income security to the portfolio, record the name and interest rate (example: US Treas. 2.5%) in the first available row in the appropriate credit quality portion of the fixed income sheet. Enter the total face value (example: 25,000 or 25) in the correct maturity column. There is one exception to putting the value in the stated maturity column: if the security has a call redemption feature, place the security value in the year of potential redemption rather than in the maturity year. Why? Because the portfolio should not have unpleasant cash flow surprises. If a bond or preferred stock paying high interest is called away prematurely, and that risk has not been accounted for, it will put a serious crimp in your total return strategy. If interest rates fall, any security with a redemption feature and a higher interest rate will likely be redeemed early by the company. This early redemption can disrupt carefully planned portfolio cash flow. By knowing when the security can be suddenly redeemed, you plan a maturity distribution to minimize the redemption effect on the fixed-income portfolio and cash flow.

The strategy for adding maturities to the portfolio depends on the market yield of the ten-year US Treasury note. Why? The ten-year treasury is considered the benchmark interest rate security for many different markets, including mortgage rates, stock values, real estate values, and other fixed-income markets. This is the strategy for building the fixed-income maturity distribution:

1. If the ten-year treasury has a yield of under 3 percent, invest only in fixed-income securities with less than four-year maturities.

2. If the ten-year treasury has a yield between 3.1 and 4 percent, place fixed-income securities in the portfolio with maturities of five to twelve years.

3. If the ten-year treasury has a yield between 4.1 and 6.5 percent, place securities in the portfolio with maturities of thirteen to twenty-five years.

4. When the ten-year treasury yields over 6.5 percent, place all new fixed-income investments in maturities of twenty-six to thirty years.

5. If the ten-year treasury yields above 7 percent, swap all fixed-income securities with maturities less than three years for thirty-year maturity and corporate preferred stocks with yields above 8 percent (examine the redemption call feature on the preferred stocks).

6. Depending on the economy and inflation, ten-year treasury yields above 6.5 percent may cause a significant decline in stock prices. When the ten-year treasury yield of 6.5 percent is accompanied by a stock market decline pressuring portfolio common stock to be at or less than 55 percent of your portfolio, split all contributions and income reinvestment: 50 percent to common stocks and 50 percent to fixed-income securities.

7. Once a fixed-income security is in the portfolio, hold it to maturity unless the credit rating falls below BBB- or interest rates are high enough (see #5 above) for the swapping of short maturities for long maturities.

Think the ten-year US Treasury note will never yield above 3.5 percent? Don't worry, it will. It's important for you to not make judgments about the level or direction of interest rates. Follow the market's lead. Use these yield benchmarks to allocate fixed-income assets. Eventually, your portfolio will have investments along the entire maturity spectrum. That's your total return strategy fixed-income goal: steady and high cash flow.

There are two primary risks to a fixed-income portfolio: credit quality and inflation. By following this fixed-income strategy, you minimize credit quality risk. Junk bonds, less than investment grade, will pay more interest, sometimes a lot more. The higher interest allure is tempting, but the goals of fixed-income investing are obtaining annual cash flow, reducing overall portfolio volatility, and receiving the initial investment back. Investors stick with investment-grade securities.

You cannot eliminate inflation risk from a fixed-income portfolio. The strategy outlined above reduces inflation risk in two ways: (1) securities mature regularly, with the proceeds reinvested at higher rates if inflation persists, and (2) using the ten-year treasury yield benchmark to determine fixed-income asset maturity selection is essentially using the Investment Pricing Pendulum, selecting longer maturities when inflation fear is high and short maturities when the bond market ignores inflation risk. Since the ten-year treasury note is considered the benchmark yield for virtually all other investment markets, the higher the yield, the more credit and inflation risk fear is embedded in the fixed-income markets. If interest rates are arbitrarily suppressed by the authorities both credit and inflation risks are forced onto the creditor. This pendulum strategy will minimize your portfolio's volatility from being caught in subsequent rate hikes.

There is a large group of speculators, including some fixed-income MFs and ETFs, who use the fixed-income market to seek not only current income but also capital gains. They do this by taking two approaches to the market. First, they select fixed-income securities that pay a low stated interest rate. Second, they select long maturity dates. In both cases, when interest rates change, these securities' price volatility will be greater than that of your fixed-income securities. Trading fixed-income securities with a focus on price volatility is the opposite of your hold-to-maturity strategy.

One last fixed-income principle: for each maturity date, pick a security with the highest stated interest rate without paying more than the par (face) value of the security.

Rule 18: Build an Effective Common Stock Strategy

Owning stock in well-run companies is a necessary risk to gain the opportunity for investment income and potential capital appreciation.

Many speculators take risks without understanding the relationship between those risks and the potential reward, consistently underestimating risks and overestimating potential rewards. Investors attempt to eliminate unnecessary risks and minimize necessary risks. One effective way to do this is to keep the Investment Pricing Pendulum in focus when selecting investments, particularly common stocks. **Rule 6** explained that every share price is composed of the current intrinsic value of the company and the market's attitude about that intrinsic value. When a company's stock is viewed favorably by speculators, the amount of market optimism in the share price increases, pushing the share price higher and away from the current intrinsic value.

Investors realize getting rich and staying rich requires a total return strategy and a method of building a portfolio that captures the cycles of fear and greed at every level, including in economic sectors and asset classes. Here is how to do it. Foremost, understand common stocks are not just pieces of paper or blips on a computer screen that go up and down. Buying well-operating businesses at a fair price based on the companies' current intrinsic value is what an investor wants. Common stocks represent partial ownership in operating companies that sell goods and services to other businesses and consumers. The companies have tangible and intangible assets, employees, and competition with other companies. The tangible worth of a company is easy to determine by looking at its book value. What is not easy to ascertain are the intangible assets' values to the company. If the company has special patents, proprietary software, brand loyalty, highly competent management, or some other unique attribute that influences its market presence, judging the value of each of these factors and assigning them a precise number is not possible. Therefore, it's best to let the market show you a range for a fair price of the stock. Dividend yield and certain company fundamental operating results for the past five years or longer, expressed as return on investment (ROI), are guidelines.

When investors own a stock, they own a portion of that company and will reap whatever rewards come to that company through profits. **Think like an owner, not just an investor.** As an investor, it is important to keep this mindset. Why? Because companies' operations are cyclical and in the next recession, profits may be down, leading to speculators selling stocks, resulting in share prices declining. Owners do not sell their ownership in companies because the company has a poor year and the stock declines. Why? Because as owners, not speculators, they are confident the economy and the company will recover.

When thinking like an owner, you want to own companies with management and operations that inspire confidence. How can you build that confidence? By examining past business results. This concept is key: invest in specific, individual companies with an operational history and, in most cases, management with the experience and confidence in the company and its operational capacity to share the profits with shareholders by paying regular dividends. Most analysts and speculators use unknowable guesses about a company's future, even incorporating guidelines given by management, who also don't have the ability to predict the future. All they can do is guess. What you, an investor, can know is how management has operated the company's core business in the past. Looking backward will give you a better understanding of management's competence than hearing them talk about how rosy the future will be. Has management demonstrated their skills in the past? Have they been able to adapt to economic changes? Initially, you may have only five years of operating history; however, every year you continue this strategy, you will build an invaluable picture of the company and its management.

Speculating with common stocks is fun. Sitting in front of multiple computer screens blinking in various colors for hours gives a speculator a sense of being in control. It appeals to the greed emotion in participants.

Investors understand stock prices will fluctuate, and they use the price volatility to their advantage. By being patient, knowing the price range they want to pay for the companies they want to own, and making investments only at these attractive valuations rather than overpaying, they reap the rewards.

— RULE 18 —

Common stock strategy:
- Invest in all macroeconomic sectors.
- Average 3% dividend return on cost.
- Use the Investment Pricing Pendulum to select stocks.
- Hold investments for at least 10 years.

The aim of investing is to get rich and stay rich, not to have fun. Fun can be a side effect of getting and staying rich, and it usually is as your portfolio and its income stream grow over time, but it should not be the primary goal. Make no mistake: a total return investment strategy, using the principles discussed in these nineteen rules, will grow over the long term. Market volatility will cause your portfolio's value to fluctuate, but the combination of investing at a price near current intrinsic value, buying individual companies you select and have confidence in, generating steady portfolio cash flow, having fixed-income securities, and holding investments for ten years or maturity will give the potential for sustained portfolio growth. The central bottom line to getting rich and staying rich is buying investments at prices below, at, or close to their current intrinsic value and holding them as the dollar value depreciates due to inflation, the economy grows, and the businesses generate more profits and dividends, thus increasing intrinsic value.

In **Rule 5** the question was asked: Should an investor sell a stock bought at a low price after it has appreciated over the years? The appreciation had two causes:

1. the company's operations improving with higher revenues, operating earnings, and cash flow

2. the market's opinion of the company's current and future competitive position

During periods when the market is dominated by greed, the value attributed to (2) will increase, moving the share price higher. When the market is dominated by fear, the value of (2) will decline; however, the increased value attributed to (1) will not. So, the correct question is this: what can replace the appreciated stock with the same potential for capital gains and dividend increases? If the appreciated stock is sold, the capital gains tax will be paid from the proceeds, so the net after-tax proceeds must be reinvested in a company that has the same characteristics as the appreciated stock did, with the same potential. Why not keep the appreciated shares and use the portfolio's dividends and interest, as well as your future contributions, to invest in another well-run company? Sure, the appreciated company's shares will be volatile, and in the next market downturn, shares will fall in price, but it's unlikely the stock will return to the original cost since the company's operations have grown over the prior years, adding to the intrinsic value. That's the point: a part of the price rise is from higher current intrinsic value. Finding good companies for investment is considered difficult. It isn't.

Many investing books speak of diversification, while many successful speculators speak of concentrated positions. Let's look at both concepts and how they fit into your efforts to accumulate and keep wealth. The easiest advice to refute is the adage "Put all your eggs in one basket and watch the basket carefully." That makes sense in some areas of life, where you have substantial control over the factors influencing the outcome of the endeavor. Owning common stocks is not something you have much control over. There is one factor that's crucial: you can control the price you pay for the investment. Otherwise, the uncontrollable and unknowable variables influencing the company and the stock market are too plentiful.

You are investing your family's hard-earned wealth. You want to minimize the necessary risks by selecting the relationship between current intrinsic value and price paid. Believing you know and can judge what else will influence the company's share price in the future is taking unnecessary risks. You can't know, so why risk everything on a few companies?

Many people have different ideas about the definition of diversification. Some want to use a broad index. Others want to invest in companies from different countries. Some believe using a lot of companies from the same economic sector gives diversification. None of these definitions lead to consistent long-term opportunities other than just getting along with mediocre performance.

Your total return strategy will give you the opportunity to have multiple investments that will perform above your expectations, and, with those that don't, you will have some cash flow from dividends to use in seeking other good investments. This diversification in your total return strategy will help smooth out the inherent volatility of the stock market.

Your goals and your strategy for achieving them have features of both a diversified strategy and a concentrated strategy. Your total return strategy will encompass companies from each of the macroeconomic sectors, giving you wide exposure to the cyclical aspects of economic growth (diversification). At the same time, you will have a concentrated set of principles and benchmarks for selecting the companies from these diverse sectors. In other words, you will not add second-rate or outright mismanaged companies to your portfolio simply in the name of diversification. Every company in your portfolio will have an opportunity to contribute to the portfolio in its own way. You'll fit them together for your unique situation, and each company will have the potential to increase its own intrinsic value over time.

Investment market segmentation is important to you on your road to lifelong wealth. There are many indices covering various segments of the stock market. If you stop and think about it, buying an index does not make sense. Indices by their nature include broad segments of the stock market, including some companies that are not operated efficiently and other companies that are high-risk businesses and may not be operating in the future. For an investor, what is important is finding and selecting companies that are good businesses with competent management and a reasonable price relative to their current intrinsic value. Indices are a place to look for candidates for your personal universe of companies.

The first step is to select an index that contains the types of companies you want, and then select the right companies for you from the index. Think of it this way: if you had all the money in the world, what companies would you want to own? You should concentrate on two indices for selecting individual companies: the S&P 500, an index of the five hundred largest US stocks, and the S&P 400, an index of mid-sized US companies. Both indices contain the types of companies you want to own, as well as those you don't. Within all indices, Wall Street divides the economy into *macroeconomic* sectors. This makes sense. There are eleven macroeconomic sectors:

1. Materials
2. Communication Services
3. Consumer Discretionary
4. Information Technology
5. Industrial
6. Real Estate

7. Utilities
8. Health Care
9. Consumer Staples
10. Energy
11. Finance

Since there are nine hundred stocks in these two indices you will choose companies from, and therefore many more than necessary for building your list of possible companies for your portfolio, select a target of one hundred companies. Want to stop with fewer companies? That's up to you; just make sure you have a reasonable spread among all of the sectors. The number of companies you select from a particular sector is personal. This allocation is just a suggestion. If you want to select fifteen from a sector, fine—just reduce the numbers in some other sectors so the total adds up to a hundred or whatever smaller number you have chosen. Consider picking the hundred stocks in the sectors as follows:

Materials – 9

Communication Services – 7

Consumer Discretionary – 10

Information Technology – 12

Industrial – 12

Utilities – 6

Health Care – 12
Consumer Staples – 12
Energy – 6
Finance – 9
Special Situations – 5

Why change Real Estate to Special Situations? Your primary residence is your real estate investment. When the time comes that you want to own more real estate, you may want to find another real estate investment you can own 100 percent of. In the meantime, the Special Situation category will allow you to seek and hold a few companies that do not fit the normal benchmarks and principles of the total return strategy. Don't worry about the special situations now—that category is for unique opportunities you find over time.

Selecting the potential portfolio stocks from the indices' nine hundred is next. Your first criterion in the selection process will be the fact that the company pays a dividend. At this point, don't worry about knowing anything else about any of the companies. Don't worry about the current stock price or the amount of the dividend, just the fact the companies you select pay a dividend. Management's competence and confidence to pay their shareholders a dividend is key. You will refine this search as you examine operational factors and build your own knowledge and confidence, but this is the right place to start. Use your brokerage firm's online research to obtain a list of companies in each index's sectors. Another way to obtain a sector's list of companies is to google "Components of S&P 500/400 (choose an index) (choose a sector)." Now for the fun part.

The easiest way to build comparable information about companies is to use a set of Excel sheets. You already have a workbook started with the fixed-income sheet. You will now add more sheets to the same workbook. Go to Appendix A. It explains the simple (they really are simple) steps to creating the sheets you need. First, set up a sheet in the Excel workbook that will alert you when the stock price of one or more of your companies reaches a point where an investment in the company would have a dividend yield of either 3 or 4 percent. If the dividend changes in the future, all you need to do is change the dividend amount in the second column of the Excel table and the target investment prices will change automatically in columns three and four.

Why set it up this way? Two reasons. First, you want the common stock portion of the portfolio to generate an average annual dividend of 3 percent based on the portfolio costs. That doesn't mean every stock will pay 3 percent, just that the mix of companies and the amount invested in each will average this target. For instance, perhaps you want to own a technology company paying only a 2 percent dividend. You can make that investment while investing a similar amount in a stock in a different sector that pays a 4 percent dividend, and thus the two investments will average a 3 percent dividend yield (2% + 4% / 2 = 3%). Second, if the stock market valuations are high, the dividend yield for most good companies will be less than 3 percent. That in itself is an indication the valuations are high, and you should wait patiently until the market, the sector, or the company comes under price pressure and gives you an opportunity to buy its stock at a price closer to the current intrinsic value and a dividend equal to or above a 3 percent yield. While the overall portfolio target yield from common stock dividends is 3 percent, each sector's target dividend yield is different.

Using the 3 to 4 percent alert level helps you understand which companies may be entering a price range close to their current intrinsic value. As shown in Appendix A, you can customize each sector's dividend alert level. For instance, electric utilities and some telephone companies in the Communication Services sector, when priced close to their current intrinsic value, have dividends at the 5 to 6 percent level, so when their dividend is only 3 percent, the share price is far above the current intrinsic value. Likewise,

Technology sector companies rarely have a 3 percent yield. When the stocks are under pressure, a 2 or 2.5 percent yield is likely. You can adjust your Excel dividend sheet for each sector (Appendix A shows how). When examining an individual company, look back at the low price each year (use charts available from your brokerage online research for determining low prices) and compare the low price to the dividend paid that year. You will quickly get a sense of what dividend level becomes attractive for that stock.

The ongoing value of this workbook sheet showing target stock prices at the 3 and 4 percent dividend levels comes from (a) the ability it gives you to change the stocks' dividends when the company changes the dividend amount, thus changing target prices, and (b) its guidance (there are other guides) as to the potential fair price level in a time of serious market crisis. Many analysts and market observers look at the amount a stock has declined from its all-time high price to seek a point of fair value. This is not logical. If the all-time high was created due to excessive greed, it has no relationship to value. A decline of 50 percent might still leave the company overvalued. The dividend yield, compared to prior valuations, and the current intrinsic value, not a hoped-for future intrinsic value, will minimize your company selection mistakes.

Surprisingly, this simple dividend requirement is more of an investment strategy than most market participants use. You are on your way to being an investor and seeking the unique potential wealth accumulation and returns available to investors.

By using an owner's mindset, you will invest in companies you are confident will sustain themselves and grow with the economy over at least a ten-year period. The importance of owning companies you select because you have confidence they will survive any market volatility cannot be overemphasized. If a company's stock price drops 40 percent, you know it will still be operating one, five, ten, or twenty years from now, so you are less likely to join the panic and sell the stock. You are more likely to use your investment income and contributions to add more shares when the price is fair based on current intrinsic value and a high dividend yield. Investors who craft their own portfolios of individual stocks will avoid realized losses due to panicky selling and spend their efforts adding new investments at fair prices.

Once a personal universe of stocks spread across the economic sectors is selected, the next step is easier. Your brokerage firm's research department should allow clients to set up a group of charts for selected stocks. A chart is a line drawing of the closing price of a stock over a specified period. There are other chart types, but this is the only type you need. Charts can be set up in a daily, weekly, or monthly format. You should set up charts in a weekly format for at least ten years. Why? Since the weekly closing price of a stock represents the momentary balance of supply and demand for the shares, this information gives you a snapshot of the market psychology toward the company at each chart point. There is another benefit: your brokerage firm may have charts that let you move a line across the chart and pinpoint the prices at the highs and lows. This is useful in working with your Excel sheets and determining dividend yields in the past.

What does the chart tell an investor? A lot and little at the same time. Remember, no one can predict the future. When a low price on the chart is followed by a higher price, or a high price is followed by a low price, it is proof that no one can predict the future. Keep that in mind.

Charts are a second way to minimize unnecessary risk as well as a starting point in understanding the present market's opinion of a company's current intrinsic value. If you want to invest in a company, you should look first at the current price relative to where it has been in the past, as shown on these weekly charts. Is the current price near the past low prices—less than 50 percent of the distance between prior highs and lows? Over a long period, such as the ten years on your chart, the high price on the chart represents the market's optimistic assessment of the company and guesses at positive improvements in the company's future. Conversely, the low price each year represents the market's pessimistic opinion of the company and its negative future prospects. The low price is dominated by fear and therefore is closer to or below the company's current intrinsic value. Now, look at the Investment Pricing Pendulum. If the current price is less than the average of the past high and low prices, fear dominates the price, meaning you may have an interest in owning the stock. If the price is higher than 50 percent, the pendulum is on the greed side and the risks are higher. Using the high and low price range over a long time frame as a gauge for the level of fear and greed in the share price gives you a sense of a fair price for the company. Waiting patiently for the right relationship between dividend yield, market fear and greed sentiment, and fundamental current intrinsic value helps you invest objectively.

Patience is an investment principle. Investing by buying a company at a fair price and holding it for ten years requires patience. With patience, you are planting seeds of potential future capital gains while building annual cash flow from dividends.

After getting a sense of the market's current opinion by setting up these online charts and finding a dividend yield benchmark, it's important to examine the companies' operational information to get a proximation of the company's current intrinsic value. What is meant by having a "sense"? Many market participants look for precision in numbers to make investment decisions. Precision is a false premise in finding companies worthy of being in your portfolio. Dividend yield, chart position, operational results expressed as ROI, and peer comparison paint a picture of stability, success, and quality. You will recognize a good investment by all of these characteristics. You are interested in a company's value now. Competent management and well-run operations will take care of the future. What you, from the perspective of an owner, want to know is what the company's operations have been like in the past during good and bad economic times. Use your brokerage firm's research department. It should offer you company financial information at the end of every fiscal year (usually the last day of December, but not necessarily) for at least five years. If the information is available for ten years, that's better, but five years is a good starting point.

The economic sector sheets in the Excel workbook (see Appendix A) are where you can compare your chosen companies within each sector. This is important. Comparing the companies in the same economic sector will highlight their management and operational quality compared to their peers. Having multiple opportunities in a sector teaches you how to distinguish each company's management quality. You don't need complicated information to begin minimizing unnecessary risks. The information you want is easy to find and use. It is readily available online from your brokerage firm's research department or determined with simple calculations in your Excel sheets. The brokerage firm's research pages for each stock should have the critical information you need listed on the Income Statement page and the Balance Sheet page. Go to the research pages online for one of your chosen companies. Look for the following information.

OI/EBIT: operating income or earnings before interest and taxes, found on the Income Statement. This is the income the company produces every year by selling its core goods or services. It is different from the net income that Wall Street and many analysts look at when discussing a price/earnings ratio. You will use this operating income information as the basis for several calculations that tell you whether the stock price is right for adding the company to the portfolio.

DWAS: diluted weighted average shares outstanding, found on the Income Statement. An owner would use the diluted shares because this number considers any options or warrants that may have been granted to employees or others. The number may change each year if the company is buying back shares in the open market or issuing new shares or options. It's important to examine the trend in DWAS to see if shareholders' value is being diluted by management's actions.

SP: share price. If it's not given, use the chart to determine the end of the fiscal year share price. You can google the share price on the specific date of the statement, or, if your brokerage firm has charts, you can click on the chart and get the price there. A third way is to go to the company's website and get the information from the Investor Relations section. The benefit of the Excel sheet is that you can substitute any share price you want, and it will change certain calculations to show good value or not. For historical comparison, it's easy to use end-of-year prices.

MKT VAL: market value of the shareholder equity, obtained by multiplying **DWAS** by **SP**. The Excel sheet is set up to do the calculation automatically once you enter the DWAS and SP. You can change this value by substituting a different price or DWAS. Using the latest DWAS and the current SP will be part of the important calculation for *current enterprise value.*

TOT DEBT: total debt for the firm, found on the Balance Sheet.

CASH/STI: cash and short-term investments of the company at the end of the fiscal year, found on the Balance Sheet.

ENT VAL: enterprise value. Theoretically, this is the price an investor or owner would pay to buy the entire company. It makes sense because if an investor bought every share, they would also have to assume all the debt, but could use the cash and short-term investments on the balance sheet to help pay for the company. While many brokerage firms may show this number for the current price and day, it is helpful to understand the enterprise value at the end of a fiscal year. Your Excel sheet has the formula for calculating automatically this number once you entered the numbers for the end of the year:

MKT VAL + TOT DEBT − CASH/STI

You can calculate the ENT VAL by using end-of-year numbers for MKT VAL or even the annual high/low numbers. The various options will guide you to a fair price range for the company.

ROI: return on investment. Your Excel sheet automatically calculates this percentage when you enter the other numbers. If you buy a stock at the price in SP above and the ENT VAL and the OI/EBIT imputed, the percentage ROI is determined. This number shows you what your return will be if the company continues to operate at the level it does now. Part of this return will come to you as dividends and part as the company's retained earnings for growing its operations and intrinsic value. There are several ways you want to use these numbers and calculations.

Look at the OI/EBIT trend over the past five years. You can examine a longer period if the numbers are available. Pay attention to how each number changes. Does the OI/EBIT fluctuate or rise each year? If it's volatile, you may want to seek a higher ROI.

Look at whether DWAS is increasing, stable, or decreasing. Ideally, you want the DWAS steady to decreasing. If it's increasing, you may look at OI/EBIT to see if the increase in shares is translating into higher OI/EBIT. Management could be using shares to develop more divisions or buy other companies. A quick look at the investor relations segment of the company's website may give the answer.

Look at whether TOT DEBT is increasing, holding steady, or decreasing. Does increasing TOT DEBT reflect higher OI/EBIT or decreasing DWAS as the company buys shares in the open market by borrowing more money? Perhaps management has set up a new division or bought another company using debt rather than shares or cash.

Look at the trend in CASH/STI. Sometimes management will park excess cash from the sale of a division, higher OI/EBIT, or new borrowings until they utilize the funds. Some activist speculators push management to either pay a larger dividend or buy back more shares in the open market when CASH/STI builds up. It takes competent and confident management to resist these short-term-oriented speculators.

Look at ENT VAL for the best picture of the markets' opinion of a company. It has two components: (1) the stock market's attitude toward the company now, and (2) the net debt the company owes (TOT DEBT – CASH/STI). Your worksheet shows you the net debt as a percentage of ENT VAL. If net debt is increasing, is it because the stock price is declining or because management is using more leverage? You have already had an opportunity to assess whether the company's share price is dominated by fear or greed. If TOT DEBT is stable and the SP is dominated by fear, you may be interested in owning the shares.

Look at the ROI range. There will always be a ROI at any level of OI/EBIT and ENT VAL. The best way to look at an ROI range is to start with the end-of-year ROI and then substitute the year's high and low prices in the calculation. Do this for each of the last five years. If your brokerage research doesn't give you the high and low, obtain the prices from the charts or go to the company website's Investor Relations section and get it there. With the three ROI calculations for a year, you can develop a range for the markets' attitude toward the company. Substitute the current SP in the last year's set of numbers and you can compare the current ROI with the historical range you just developed, giving you a sense of the attractiveness of the investment. The more fear in the MKT VAL, the higher the ROI. Keep in mind, the ROI you accept for each investment will impact your AAIR and AATC for compounding the returns of your portfolio.

Let's see what these numbers tell you. The past numbers will give you a sense of the company's actual operational performance and what the market thought about the company's operations at various times. This knowledge is important to an owner since those results can be compared with other companies' ROIs in the same economic sector for the same year. By using the charts and developing the numbers for annual high and low ROI in conjunction with the Investment Pricing Pendulum, an investor can obtain a better sense of how the current stock price is influenced by fear or greed. The whole process helps you understand the share's price relative to its current intrinsic value.

Getting rich and staying rich, with a total return strategy, uses benchmarks designed to avoid increasing greed in the marketplace. Many speculators use relative factors that change with the markets, even if those factors are manipulated, such as interest rates, or are completely uncoupled from current intrinsic value. These factors entice more greed the higher the markets climb, allowing users to justify new investments at prices far above the current intrinsic value. Your total return and pendulum investing strategy uses fixed measurements that act as guideposts: certain yields of the ten-year treasury dictate the maturities selected in the portfolio's fixed-income portion. ROI targets based on current intrinsic value and dividend levels signal a time to invest in individual companies. If the dividend yield or ROI is out of fair return range as demonstrated by history, you don't make the investment. What these standards do is help minimize risks by signaling times when valuations indicate you should or should not be active in the markets. Your total return strategy assists you in recognizing the times to build liquidity and wait patiently for when fear dominates the markets, sectors, or companies.

Now that you have a method for determining a fair price for a company, the question is this: How much should you invest in each stock? Diversifying the right way with patience is critical. Start by knowing you eventually want to have several common stock investments in each of the economic sectors. You can't achieve this goal all at one time. Each investment should initially be no more than 2 percent of portfolio value in each stock. When the portfolio is small, this may seem like it's not worthwhile. It is. Consistent wealth accumulation depends on building a balanced portfolio. Putting too much money in a small number of stocks in the beginning raises unnecessary risks. Your goal is to have dividend-paying stocks in each of the major economic sectors, thereby using the economy's dynamic cyclical nature to smooth out your portfolio volatility.

When one sector is performing well, those sector companies in the portfolio will participate. When a sector is out of favor in the marketplace and the companies' share prices decline, you can build up the portfolio in that sector by adding companies. Over time, as the economy

———— ◆ ————

evolves, one sector or another will outpace the others. This is natural. The sector will increase its percentage of the portfolio. You want to reinvest your investment income and contributions in other sectors that are lagging. In this way, you participate in what the market is focused on while building areas of your portfolio that have the potential to be market leaders as the economy changes. It takes time to accumulate positions in all sectors (unless the whole market is under extreme pressure in a crisis). The compounding of a total return strategy will be enhanced by the annual investment cash flow and by a good balance among the sectors in the portfolio.

This brings us to a point about market dynamics, which are the natural cycles the markets exhibit. The market gives investing opportunities on a regular basis:

- Every year one or two economic sectors or companies come under intense negative price pressure because of economic cycle changes or company specific issues. This selling pressure causes company shares in the sector to decline as much as 10 percent.
- Every two or three years, the stock market is subject to changes in speculative psychology because of economic news or some other events that surprise market participants. These negative adjustments can

bring the market indices down as much as 15 to 20 percent.

- At least once a decade, when the positive excesses in the stock market have reached a high point, negative events can send the indices down 50 percent (2000 and 2008) to 90 percent (early 1930s).

These are the times you can add companies in every sector to your portfolio at prices for which rewards far outweigh risks. Understanding these cyclical forces is how you can be ready to add to your portfolio when the prices are fair.

You will be prepared for market opportunities by having set up the TARGET DIV PRICE sheet and the SECTOR OPERATIONS sheets. These sheets alert you to the price range in which your stocks achieve fair value. A word about that fair price: when a market has had a long run upward and begins to roll over, the market leaders lead the way down. Many analysts and media believe the stocks become a good value if they decline 40 or even 50 percent. That doesn't make sense. The prior high may have been due to excessive greed, leading to an excessive valuation. Even if a stock has declined significantly, the decline percentage is no indication it is worthy of being added to your portfolio. By using the metrics discussed here, you can find the fair price range and determine the right price.

Once you understand a range of prices in which the investment is a fair value, place a good-till-canceled, limit-price order to buy half the amount of stock you want at the fair price range top. Enter a similar order for the other half at the bottom of the fair price range. Repeat this procedure for companies in different economic sectors. If every order is executed, make sure you have money available to pay for the investments. By using this strategy, instead of panicking in a market crash, you will be in the unique position of gaining portfolio value as the market declines. Buying when the market, sector, or company is under stress is what will solidify your family's total return strategy and help you get rich and stay rich.

Rule 19: Use Careful Tax Strategies

The most important tax rule to remember is "Don't let the tax tail wag the investment strategy dog." Placing investments, when possible, in the most tax-efficient account is the most important tax strategy (**Rule 8**). As an investor and owner of good companies in your taxable account, selected by you, and held for ten or more years to minimize taxes, you may have a reason to sell assets. The gain is taxed at the capital gains rate. There is a tax strategy to keep in mind called *tax swapping*. If you take a profit in any investment asset (not your personal residence), you should look at your portfolio and see if you have a security in the taxable accounts (non-retirement accounts) selling below the price

— **RULE 19** —

Don't let the tax tail wag the
investment strategy dog.

paid for it. If so, you can sell as many shares as necessary of that stock to offset all or part of the realized gain. This strategy will eliminate or reduce the amount of taxes due on any realized gain. There is one important tax factor to keep in mind: if you sell a stock for a loss and use the loss to reduce taxes, you must wait at least thirty-one days before buying the stock back. After thirty-one days, you should reinvest in the company if the reason for initially owning the stock is still valid. Remember, it is more important to allow the portfolio to compound returns rather than to save taxes now, so don't let a small tax savings interrupt your portfolio strategy.

Get Rich and Stay Rich

Following these simple rules, investors will achieve their financial goals, not just at retirement, but at every phase of life. Wealth and income grow from this disciplined investment approach even as market volatility reflects changing economic activity. If the investment markets become overvalued, these principles will alert you, and you will begin building liquid investment reserves for the inevitable downturn. When markets are undervalued, portfolio investments will decline, but you will have the resources to take advantage of the market decline, adding companies at fair value and a good dividend yield. The total return strategy and rules are not hard to understand, they don't require significant sacrifices, and, once your Excel sheets are set up, they do not require large amounts of time.

Be patient, be disciplined, and enjoy the rewards!

Appendix A

Here's how to set up a portfolio analysis workbook:

1. Open Excel and click on New Blank Workbook.

2. Go to the bottom of the blank sheet, to the Sheet 1 tab. Right-click and select "Rename." Write "Fixed-Inc Mat" and then hit Enter.

3. Skip columns A and B. Starting with column C, in row 1, enter this year's date and the next 40 years' dates in consecutive columns.

4. Go back to column A. In row 2, write AAA.

5. Skip the next ten rows. In column A, row 13, enter AA.

6. Skip five rows (there aren't many AA bonds). In column A, row 19, enter A.

7. Skip twelve rows. In column A, row 32, enter BBB.

8. Save the Fixed-Inc Mat sheet.

The fixed-income spreadsheet is now ready for you to enter security information and maturities in the proper columns (see **Rule 17**).

Next, use the circled + at the bottom center of Sheet 1 to add a second sheet. Title this page **Target Div. Price** (see step 2 above for renaming a sheet) and press Enter.

Your Excel Portfolio Workbook

Sheet 1: Fixed-Income Quality and Maturity

Sheet 2: Common stock target prices for 3% and 4% dividend yields

Sheets 3–13: One sheet for each sector's common stocks valuation analysis

Since you will need only four columns per economic sector, this page will be set up with three sectors spread along the columns as well as rows. Set up the first sector this way:

1. In column A, row 1, enter the word SYMBOL. In column B, row 1, enter DIV. In column C, row 1, enter 3% PRICE. In column D, row 1, enter 4% PRICE. This sector is now set up.

2. Go to columns H thru K and set up another sector the same way you did in columns A thru D.

3. Go to columns P thru S and set up a third sector.

4. Go back to column A, row 34. Set up three more sectors in columns A-D, H-K, and P-S, just like the first three.

5. Repeat these setups in row 65 and row 86 until all eleven sectors have a place on the sheet.

6. Save your work.

Now, follow these steps to populate the sector classifications with stocks:

1. In Columns A, H, and P, row 2, under the word SYMBOL, name the economic sectors (Materials, Health Care, etc.), placing one sector in each of the eleven tables.

2. In columns C, J, and R, row 2 and corresponding lower rows in each table, enter the following formula: =B3/0.03.

3. In columns D, K, and S, row 2 and corresponding lower rows in each table, enter the formula: =B3/0.04.

4. In columns A, H, and P, row 3, enter the symbol for the first stock in the sector. For example, in the Utility sector, you might have SO for Southern Company. Complete the rest of sector table with stocks.

5. In columns B, I, and Q, row 3 and corresponding lower rows, enter the current annual dividend for the stocks in each of the sectors' table.

HINT

When placing the formulas in the appropriate columns, enter the first one and make sure it works. Then right-click on the box. The original box should have a dotted line around it. Click on copy. Click the box, hold the cursor down, and drag down the column for the rows in that sector table. The new boxes should be highlighted gray. Right-click and select Paste. Each box should have the appropriate formula for that row.

What will happen is the Excel columns C, J, and R will divide the dividend in columns B, I, and Q by 3 percent, giving a stock price for which, the current dividend will be a yield of 3 percent. In columns D, K, and S, the dividend in Column B, I, and Q will be divided by 4 percent, giving a target price at that yield. Do this for each sector grouping row that has a stock symbol and dividend (see HINT box for shortcut). You can change the formula in the appropriate column as needed if a sector does not have the potential for a 3 or 4 percent dividend. For instance, during major market selloffs, the Tech sector may yield only 2 or 2.5 percent. Go to the appropriate row for that stock and the column with the 3 percent formula. Change the formula by switching the 0.03 divisor to 0.02. In the next column, change the 0.04 to 0.025. New target prices will reflect the changes. Likewise, two sectors (Utilities and Communication Services) have some stocks for which their yield during a market selloff may be in the 5 to 6 percent range. Just change the formula numbers to 0.05 and 0.06 in the columns. When a company changes its dividend, up or down, just change the amount in the dividend column and the target prices will automatically change. Don't forget to save your work as you go along.

Now it's time to set up additional analysis sheets in your Excel workbook. This time you will set up one sheet for each economic sector. Use the circled + at the bottom center of a sheet to create new sheets, one at a time, for each sector. Rename each new sheet with a sector name. Why one sheet per sector? A sector has unique economic influences that impact most, if not all, companies in that sector. It's important to compare the available investments in each sector since these companies have similar economic and social influences on their businesses. By seeing all companies in the sector together, you will begin to differentiate the fair value of each company. Here are the steps for each sector sheet:

1. Start at column C, row 1, with year dates going back at least five years and going forward at least twenty years. So, column C should have the past five years first. Going forward, add a year until the twenty-five columns have a date.

2. Go to column A and enter the following in each row:

Row 3	Stock symbol
Row 4	OI/EBIT
Row 5	DWAS
Row 6	SP
Row 7	MKT CAP
Row 8	TOT DEBT
Row 9	CASH/STI

Row 10	ENT VAL
Row 11	ROI
Row 12	LEV RATIO

HINT

Once the first titles of rows in column A are in place, you can highlight the rows, right-click, select Copy, and drop down to the appropriate next row (leave at least one row between stocks), then right-click and select Paste. Do this copying for each stock in the sector.

For a reminder of the meanings of these abbreviations, see **Rule 18**. All of this information is readily available in your brokerage firm's online research, except for four lines: **MKT VAL, ENT VAL, ROI** and **LEV RATIO**. These four lines are determined by adding, subtracting, multiplying, or dividing the other lines. Here is how to set up these four lines:

1. In column C, row 7, enter the formula: =C5*C6 (the * means multiply).

2. In row 10, enter the formula: =C7+C8-C9.

3. In row 11, enter the formula: =C4/C10.

4. In row 12, enter the formula =(C8-C9)/C10.

Now, when you populate the information from your brokerage research for the other rows, these four rows will automatically calculate.

HINT

When you have the correct formula in column C, place the cursor on column C, row 7, and then right-click and select Copy. The box in column C, row 7, should have a dotted line around it. Click on the box, hold down the cursor, and drag it across the sheet to the end of the row. Then right-click and select Paste. This maneuver will populate each column with the correct formula for that row.

As you add stocks to each sector sheet, make sure to use the proper row number. For instance, the second company's information will be in rows 14 through 22. See the HINT box to populate the years across a row.

Once you have one stock analysis set up, you can right-click and highlight the entire rows and columns for that one stock, select Copy, and then Paste the work farther down the sheet, skipping one row.

Setting up the workbook takes some time, but once it's set up, the perspective you get by seeing the companies' numbers along with their sector peers sharpens your investment decisions and reinforces your goals of getting rich and staying rich.

Appendix B:
Sample Investment Policy Statement

PORTFOLIO OBJECTIVE

The portfolio objective is to build wealth and keep it. To achieve these goals, the portfolio will use a total return strategy with specific criteria for income. The overall portfolio income from all investments will average 3.5% of costs. It's not possible to set a potential capital gains target.

ASSET ALLOCATION

The target asset allocation will be 70% common stocks and 30% fixed-income. All investment income and new contributions will be allocated in the same percentages unless:

(a) Common stocks are 55% or less and the ten-year US Treasury note yields less than 6.5%, at which time the investment income and new contributions will be allocated 100% to common stocks. If the ten-year treasury yields 6.5% or more and the common stocks are more than 55% of the portfolio, the investment income and new contributions will be allocated 50% to common stocks and 50% to fixed-income securities with maturities of 25 years or longer.

(b) When common stocks are 85% of the portfolio, investment income and new contributions will go 80% to fixed-income and 20% to common stocks until the asset allocation is 70% common stocks and 30% fixed-income.

PORTFOLIO ASSETS

No mutual funds, ETFs, options, or other derivatives will be used in the portfolio.

FDIC bank deposit accounts will be used for uninvested cash. Investment-grade corporate bonds and preferred stocks and US Treasury notes and bonds will be used for fixed-income investing. Common stocks of US-domiciled corporations traded on US stock exchanges will be used in the portfolio's equity portion.

TOTAL RETURN STRATEGY

The portfolio's common stocks will represent all macro-economic sectors as used in the S&P indices except for Real Estate. The common stocks will generate an average of 3% per year from dividends based on the costs of the securities. When first placed in the portfolio, no common stock will be more than 2% of portfolio value. Each common stock investment will be held for at least ten years.

All investment grade fixed-income securities that maintain their investment grade rating will be held to maturity unless a security with a short maturity is sold to be reinvested in common stocks or in longer-maturity fixed-income securities based on the fixed-income strategy. At the time they are placed in the portfolio, the fixed-income securities will have a stated interest rate or dividend equal or close to prevailing market rates, so the security's price is at or close to par or face value. Maturities to be placed in the portfolio will depend on the yield on the ten-year treasury security as follows. A treasury yield of 3% or less: maturities up to four years. A treasury yield of 3.1% to 4%: maturities of five to twelve years. A treasury yield of 4.1% to 6.5%: maturities of thirteen years to twenty-five years. A treasury yield over 6.5%: maturities of thirty years or longer.

Glossary

AAIR: average annual investment returns for a portfolio, comprised of investment income from dividends and interest and both realized and unrealized capital gains/appreciation. It can vary annually, so it's best determined over a longer period, such as five or ten years.

AATC: average annual total contributions, comprised of the AAIR added to the portfolio additions from the client and any employer matching contribution to an employer retirement account.

Account: a brokerage account for placing assets as they accumulate. There are three generic types: tax-deferred accounts, such as traditional IRAs or employer retirement accounts; tax-free accounts, such as Roth retirement accounts; and taxable accounts that have no special tax exemption, with all income and realized capital gains taxable when received.

Activist: a speculator, usually a hedge fund or even a private equity fund, that takes a position in a company's stock and pushes management to make changes under threat of a proxy fight.

Algorithm: computer code that develops specific actions in response to market movements.

Art: investing or speculating is part mathematical and part intuition, which is more art than logic.

Assets: things that are owned, such as land, machinery, patents, trademarks, and brands. In investing, there are two types of assets: liquid and illiquid. Real estate is an illiquid asset because it is time-consuming and expensive to buy or sell. Some private equity and venture capital funds are considered illiquid since they require a commitment from investors to hold the investment for ten years or longer and have no active market for any resale. Liquid investments are generally publicly traded fixed-income securities and common and preferred stocks issued by corporations that are listed on recognized exchanges. Even though the prices may change at any time, these publicly traded securities can be sold anytime the markets are open.

Brokerage financial consultant: a person who interfaces with a public client of a brokerage firm and has usually earned degrees and certifications developed to help the client understand the investing process. The professional brings together the client and other professionals, such as an SEC-registered investment advisor, to meet the client's financial criteria.

Business media: radio, television, newspaper, and internet sources of investment market news.

Capital gains/appreciation: the price movement of an asset when it becomes higher than the original price paid for the asset. Unrealized capital gains/appreciation is the amount a security has risen above the original cost price while the asset continues to be held. Realized capital gains/appreciation is when the asset has been sold for a price higher than the original price. Taxes may have to be paid on realized capital gains/appreciation.

Cash reserves: the amount of money a person or family should set aside in either one year or less FDIC-insured CDs or a US Treasury bills/notes. The amount of cash reserves should be equal to six months of salaries and bonuses, after taxes and deductions, to allow the person or family in a financial crisis to make financial decisions calmly and logically before taking assets from the investment portfolio.

CEO of portfolio: the chief executive officer of the portfolio, the client, who sets out in writing the parameters and basic strategy for achieving the portfolio's objectives within his or her own risk tolerance.

COO of portfolio: the chief operating officer, any person to whom the client has delegated authority to select the investments for the portfolio within the guidelines set by the CEO in the investment policy statement.

Common stock: ownership shares of an operating company. The common stock shareholders elect the board of directors of the company, who in turn hire management and monitor operations.

Compounding of portfolio returns: allowing the investment income and capital appreciation to be reinvested in the portfolio to stimulate more income and growth over time.

Creditor: a person or entity who lends money to another, seeking either investment income or a combination of investment income and some form of capital appreciation.

Credit rating: a rating of credit quality assigned to fixed-income securities. Investment-grade credit ratings are AAA, AA, A, and BBB. Non-investment-grade credit ratings, also called "junk" ratings, are BB, B, CCC, CC, C.

cryptocurrencies: computer entries representing an owned position. There is no tangible value, just the belief by the owner that it has some value because the owner paid real government backed money for the cryptocurrency. There are essentially two types: privately created cryptocurrencies and central bank–created digital currency. The central bank digital currency is backed in some way by the government controlling the central bank.

Current intrinsic value: the book value of a company, plus the value of its patents, trademarks, and brands; its management competency; and the overall operations of its basic business. This number cannot be definitively determined due to the intangible assets in the mix; however, a range of values can be estimated by examining the market's opinion of the company at the low share price each year in the past five to ten years and comparing those prices to the actual tangible book value. Corporate management and Wall Street analysts include in their calculation the company's expected future operation, which is unknowable and therefore distorts the current value. *See intrinsic value below.*

Debtor: an entity that borrows money. The borrowed money may be used for speculating, investing, or general purposes. Usually, the borrowed money will have a cost of interest, dividends, or possibly participation in the debtor's business. There is usually a finite period before the money must be paid back.

Decision tree process: Many analysts set up a series of decisions that have to be made or assumed to arrive at a range of outcomes when estimating the earnings or revenues of an entity being analyzed. The process can be complicated or simple with each step dependent upon the inputs in the prior step.

Derivatives: securities created by Wall Street to allow speculators to bet on the price movement or value of some other basic security, such as a common stock or a fixed-income security like a bond. Options, futures, and swaps are the principal derivatives. While some are traded on exchanges, several derivatives are privately agreed to by Wall Street firms and individual speculators. Many derivatives entail using leverage.

Discounted cash flow model: one method used by Wall Street to determine the value of a security. It depends on guesses about future operating results and interest rates, among other factors that are unknowable.

Dividend discount model: one method used by Wall Street to value securities that assumes the current dividend will be paid in the future, it will grow by an assumed amount, and the dividends over a period of time will be discounted back to the present date by an interest rate that may or may not be appropriate because of future unknowable events.

diversification: inclusion of a broad number of different securities in a portfolio. The type of diversification is as important as the number of different securities. Wall Street's idea of diversification is questionable in many cases.

Dividends: the portion of a company's operating results paid by the company's management to the company's shareholders.

Economic sector: a group of companies in similar industries. The stock market is divided into eleven macroeconomic sectors: Materials, Finance, Utilities, Health Care, Consumer Staples, Consumer Discretionary, Technology, Energy, Industrial, Communication Services, and Real Estate.

ESG: environmental, social, and governance characteristics of a company. In 2022, political activists are pushing for regulators to use these characteristics in their supervision.

Emotion: a feeling, such as fear or greed, that dominates investment markets in various degrees at any given time.

ETF: exchange-traded fund.

Fiat money: currency issued by a government without any collateral backing other than the promise to honor the currency and laws that make others accept the currency at face value.

Fintech companies: companies using technology to develop direct consumer relationships and bring consumers financial services.

Fixed-income securities: debt securities that pay interest or dividends and have a specific date when the borrower will return the lender's money at the face (par) value.

Gambling: placing bets on the outcome of an action with little or no knowledge.

Gold: a precious metal that has been used throughout the world as money in various forms for more than 2,500 years.

Hedge funds: investment pools that take risky positions in various markets, depending on the type of hedge fund, using leverage and aiming to achieve above-average returns for their investors. They charge high basic fees and a performance fee of 10 to 20 percent of the net profits. When the fund has a significant loss, it usually shuts down because it can't charge a performance fee until the fund returns to its value before the loss.

High-flying stock: a company that has become the favorite of market speculators because it is growing fast, making multiple acquisitions for growth, or introducing a new product that is highly profitable and in demand by users. Eventually, small speculators, most mutual funds, and ETFs find a way to own the stock at valuations detached from reality.

Hope-and-prayer stock: shares of a company that is financially insecure and requires some magical event to keep it from going bust. These stocks always inspire interesting and different stories of great riches in the future when some hard to imagine event happens.

Hubris: an egotistical pride exhibited by many in the investment world who believe they have a magic touch to predict the future due to their native intelligence and quantitative systems.

Inflation: a period when prices rise for a broad range of goods and services. Inflation is caused by and a direct result of monetary authorities, in the United States the Federal Reserve, deliberately debasing the currency by creating too much money, suppressing interest rates artificially, or financing deficit spending by the federal government, sometimes all three irresponsible activities. It is facilitated by fiat money and political control over the monetary authorities.

Institutional investor: anyone who manages a portfolio for someone else, including pension plan managers, mutual fund and ETF managers, hedge funds, and asset managers for other organizations in a variety of industries.

Insurance: policies to protect against certain unexpected financial losses. Most everyone needs three types: medical, life, and property. The premiums can change every year or be fixed for a certain multiple-year amount.

Intrinsic value: see *current intrinsic value* above. When most of Wall Street and corporate management speaks of intrinsic value, they are including guesses about future growth of the company.

Inverse movement: movement in opposite directions. For example, with fixed-income investments, when interest rates increase, the price of already-issued fixed-income securities will decrease. When interest rates decrease, the price of already-issued fixed-income securities will increase.

Investment goal/objective: the result a portfolio owner wants to achieve with the portfolio. There can be multiple goals, such as educating children, becoming wealthy, having more income, or securing retirement.

Investment income: the amount of cash flow each year from dividends and interest generated by the portfolio's assets. Not to be confused with realized capital gains or portfolio contributions.

IRA conversion: the process of moving some of a traditional IRA into a Roth IRA by paying current income taxes on the amount being converted, which is sometimes advantageous.

Leverage: the act of using some form of borrowing to magnify the returns to a portfolio or individual security. The simplest form of leverage is money borrowed from a creditor. In the investment markets, there are options, futures, and swaps, all derivatives that allow the speculator to put up limited amounts of money but participate in the price movement of the security the derivative is based on. The use of leverage magnifies the gains or losses experienced.

Long term: a longer period for which an investment is held by a speculator or an investor. Some Wall Street professionals believe a long-term investment is three months, while business media use the IRS definition of one year. Private equity firms set holding periods for their fund investors at seven years or longer. Investors who understand how to get rich and stay rich define the long term as ten years or more.

Loss of capital: the loss of money that occurs when an investor sells an asset that has decreased in value and is less than what he or she bought it for. There are two types of losses: temporary and permanent. Temporary losses come from owning a security that fluctuates in price and due to the volatility, the price falls below the price at which it was placed in a portfolio. Permanent losses stem from two actions. First, a speculator buys a security at a price that has no relationship to the current intrinsic value, the price falls below the original cost, and the speculator chooses to sell the investment rather than hold it. A second permanent loss is experienced when a security at a loss is either taken over by a large speculator or company at a price lower than the original cost or the company's operations fail, it goes bankrupt, and the shares become worthless.

Margin debt: debt an investor accrues by borrowing part of the cost of an investment from a broker. Brokerage firms lend to clients in amounts based on the value of the client's portfolio held at the firm and the types of securities in the account. The brokerage firm charges interest and has the right to lend the securities in the portfolio. If the portfolio value falls to a predetermined level, in a short time the client must either liquidate securities or deposit additional monies in the account. The right to lend the securities in the account is given to the brokerage firm when margin papers are signed, even if the account does not borrow any money.

Market index: a group of companies in the investment markets, segmented by Wall Street, to measure the performance of various market segments. Used to measure institutional investor performance. The Dow Jones Indices, The S&P Indices, and the Russell Indices are the most widely known indices.

Monte Carlo Simulation: a computer program designed to accept variables and show how long a person's portfolio will last in retirement. It requires guesses about the portfolio size at retirement, the average returns on the portfolio during retirement years, the inflation during retirement years, and the withdrawal requirement during retirement, none of which are knowable. Estimates that are too conservative or too liberal can seriously impact the portfolio's owner. It does not account for the potential for family emergencies that could result in additional significant withdrawals and cause the portfolio to spiral downward as regular withdrawals continue.

Maturity: the date when a fixed-income security is paid off by the borrower.

Momentum: a continual rise in the price of a security. Some speculators only buy stocks that they determine have momentum characteristics.

Mortgage: a loan collateralized with real estate. There are many types of mortgages, such as fixed-interest, adjustable-interest, or hybrid. There are many term periods of mortgages. The fixed-rate, thirty-year maturity mortgage is the safest mortgage for investors because it locks in the bulk of housing costs for a long period. Even if the real estate will likely be sold in three, five, or ten years, the thirty-year fixed-rate mortgage gives the borrower all the flexibility and control.

mutual funds: pooled investments that are professionally managed. These funds are priced every market day at the market's close. There are serious issues surrounding these funds that are detailed in regulatory required disclosure documents. *See prospectus.*

Operating income: earnings before interest and taxes, the amount of income derived from the core activities of the company.

Operational bank account: the account in which an investor deposits salary and other non-investment income and from which ordinary living expenses are paid.

Packaged securities: pools of securities, like mutual funds, ETFs, unit trusts, and various types of derivatives. Wall Street markets these packaged securities to speculators as diversifying and leveraging securities. Business media highlight these packaged securities by focusing on sector or index volatility rather than on individual securities. Many institutional investors use these securities to quickly move into or out of sectors.

Portfolio: a group of securities developed by speculators and investors to participate in various investment markets. Investors develop a portfolio designed to meet their unique wants, needs, and risk temperament.

Prospectus and additional information: two legal documents that the SEC requires mutual funds and ETFs to make available to prospective investors. Both documents have information about the risks and strategy of the funds. Anyone thinking of investing in a fund should read two sections, the stated risks and the explanation of the strategy, both of which will surprise a prospective investor who expects a simple investment.

Quantitative investing: investing decisions made by algorithms run on a computer with little or no human intervention.

Redemption call price/date: a date and price at which the issuer can require the owner of the security to turn in the security and receive the face value, and possibly a small premium, before the scheduled maturity date; a feature of many fixed-income securities other than US Treasury securities.

Registered investment advisor (RIA): a professional investor registered with the Securities Exchange Commission (SEC).

retail speculators/investors: participants in the investment markets who are not professionals.

Risk tolerance: a measurement of the type and amount of risk that speculators and investors are willing to accept when seeking capital appreciation.

Acknowledgements

I'm grateful to Mark and Betsy Friedman, Bill Pickard, and Murray Freedman for reviewing an early draft of this manuscript and giving their insightful comments.

Luke Palder and his team at Proofreading Services.com did their usual outstanding job of developmental, copy-editing, and proofreading. Any residual mistakes are mine.

Ghislain Viau of Creative Book Design did his excellent work on developing the cover and interior designs.

Thank you needs to go to my assistant Sheree Adams for keeping all the logistical work flowing between the various parties in this endeavor.

Judy, my wife, muse, motivator, and best critic read drafts, discussed clarity, and overall kept me on course to finish this project.